{ TRUE FOOD }

{ TRUE FOOD }

shift from disordered dieting to mindful eating in 40 days

explore your relationship with food and self

Beth Summers

Cover Art by Adam Borgia / Foreword by Allie Duzett

Dedicated to every eater; learn to trust yourself again.
Thank you food, for trusting me with the learning process and
helping me to remember who I am.

Contents

BODY: Sensational Dieting

MIND: Paradigm Shifting

EMOTIONS: Experiential Dining

SPIRIT: Meditative Eating

{ Foreword }

I love Beth's work.

I am an expert in the workings of the subconscious mind. Earlier this year, I teamed up with a nutritional therapy practitioner to provide a class exploring the link between the subconscious mind and physical health, focusing on using food for healing. But something was missing from my class, and it was Beth. Beth's work — and the exercises she includes in this workbook — fill an incredible gap that was missing from my class and, let's face it, is probably missing in your life.

In her introduction she talks about the importance of "triggering" food experiences as vehicles for healing. *This concept is so important I had to write this sentence in italics.* The subconscious mind is full of old emotions and troublesome belief programs, and many, many, many of them are tied to food. These are emotions and ideas tied to eating, to enjoying food, to the meal experience itself. These are emotions and ideas tied to our own physical bodies, the bodies of those around us, and even our experiences of ourselves as embodied beings.

I didn't realize how many hang-ups I myself had about food until I took my own class with Beth as a teacher! I was blown away by how many of the experiences she led us through triggered deep reactions within myself.

But this is how the subconscious mind works. The subconscious mind is full of emotions and beliefs and concerns, and they all crave one thing more than anything else: **validation**. But you can't validate something that you don't know is there!

The experiences in this workbook are exceptional because they really target both the conscious and the subconscious minds. Expect to feel things you don't expect to feel. Expect to think things you don't expect to think. Expect to breathe a little faster sometimes. This is a good experience and an important experience because these things your mind drags up can then be **validated**, honored, and then released. Once you consciously understand your subconscious emotions and triggers surrounding food, you can thank them for their service and imagine them flying away. And you know what? It may even feel like they literally do fly away. You can be left feeling physically lighter. And you may see how your entire life transforms as issues tied to food clear up and leave you feeling stronger, healthier, and more capable of listening to your heart when it comes to food choices and life choices.

The fact is that food is a fuel, and food is a tool — on top of all the other wonderful things food is. Food fuels our literal brains and bodies, and it is a tool we can use to make our bodies and minds stronger and healthier.

Use this workbook to dig deep into your own psyche; to heal; to grow; to learn important skills; to face the things in your life that may be holding you back in ways you haven't even identified yet. Use these exercises to bless your life as you take the next step in your healing journey.

—Allie Duzett, Subconscious Mind Expert
allieduzett.com

"RESPECT FOR FOOD IS A
RESPECT FOR LIFE, FOR WHO
WE ARE AND WHAT WE DO."
–THOMAS KELLER

{ Preface }

There is no good food or bad food, just food. Before you start lighting your torches and sharpening your pitch forks, just hear me out. I graduated with degrees in Health Science and Biology, with an emphasis in Health Promotion & Lifetime Wellness. I've pursued various certifications and continuing education courses, all having to do with health and wellness. The human body is fascinating to me, but food is my true passion. I love everything about it: gardening, grocery shopping, meal planning, cooking, eating, etc. My education and training taught me to label food as healthy or junk. Nutrient dense versus empty calories. Good food. Bad food.

I also happen to be a human being living in a very judgmental world. We're told every day what to eat and what not to eat and why. Don't even get me started on the dieting industry and what that's done to society's issues with objectification! Everyone I know, myself included, has some form of disordered eating. And most people are more confused than ever about what they should eat. The result: fear and shame-based eating.

When I developed weight management programs for health centers and personal clients, I created plans that incorporated as much up to date information as possible. As the years went by, I grew more and more frustrated with the process. The latest studies all seemed to contradict each other, or at very least made things more complicated. And even worse, those clients who needed help the most were "failing" — or in other words, not losing weight. Here I was, throwing the books at them, with little to no improvement. Not only were they unsuccessful in attaining their goals, but I felt like I failed them as their coach.

Eventually I switched to a more holistic approach, implementing essential oils, positive affirmations, yoga, Ayurveda and chakra balancing. These methods seemed to help some, but not others, and I continued to feel that something was missing. I also started to notice that the typical Western theory and practice of wellness, along with the various Alternative Health modalities, functioned from an outward-in approach. Both were more concerned with identifying what was wrong rather than focusing on what was right.

It wasn't until I discovered the spiritual practice of Kundalini Yoga, and really started to embrace the meaning of Sat Nam, that something inside me started to click. "I am Truth, Truth is My Identity." Everything I am, right here and right now, is enough. What an empowering and freeing thought! As I began to shift from a place of judgment to a place of acceptance for myself, I was better able to extend that courtesy to others. Everyone is doing the best they can with what they have. There is no good person or bad person, just people.

As soon as I stopped labeling myself and others, I started to recognize how often we label the world around us, including our food. Eventually I became more and more uncomfortable with the labels I had once accepted as truth from my social and educational upbringing. We aren't fighting a war against obesity, we're telling people that they're bad. And we extend that belief to the food we put in our mouths. Take a cupcake, for example. Yes, it's made with sugar, food dye, and white flour. When you hold that cupcake in your hand, what do you see? A bad food.

But what if, instead of labeling food as bad and therefore ourselves as bad because we want to eat it or because we choose to indulge, we see things differently. Someone made that cupcake. Maybe we know and love that person, and this food item was gifted to us. Maybe we don't know the person behind the treat, but I can promise it came from someone with thoughts and feelings as valid as our own. Perhaps a skilled baker who finds joy in his or her craft. And what about the ingredients that went into the making of the cupcake? Think of the cashier, the storekeeper, the harvester, the farmer. And they are people just like us, doing the best they can.

I'm not saying there isn't value in clean eating. I am not suggesting that you go and eat pizza all day, every day. What I am suggesting is that there is value in pizza simply because it exists. And while it may not always be the best option for our physical bodies, it may on occasion be a great option for our spiritual well-being. Please, by all means, find a wellness program that supports your specific nutritional needs. And as you implement your particular protocol, it's important that you remember: food is more complex than we give it credit for while still being beautifully simple in its ability to nourish our souls.

Our worth as individuals is unchanging. Take a dirty and tattered hundred dollar bill to the bank and they will still accept it as valuable currency. No matter how damaged we are, or how processed our food is, there is an inherent value that is worthwhile. And that is what I'm encouraging us to explore, to rediscover and embrace as truth.

Filling our food with harmful and unkind thoughts is far more toxic than the processed and unhealthy components that make up our food. I believe in the beauty and power of Namaste: the Light in Me recognizes the Light in You, and in that tree, and in that rock, and in that cupcake or pizza. Yes, we can raise our vibration and improve our health by eating whole foods or celebrating our body through exercise. But what if we can believe in ourselves, in the perfection of our Inner Light, in such a way that raises the vibration of the world around us? What if we can heal ourselves by healing our relationship with our food?

I find joy and meaning in the connection of all things. We all come from the same Source. My food and I are one and the same, because we are a part of a Greater Whole. From our first breath until our last, we need food for our survival. We also need it to enjoy life, by allowing our food to feed not only our physical bodies, but also our subtle bodies. For lasting health we need to balance our physical, mental, emotional and spiritual well-being. I invite you to connect with your food on every level, and discover true health for yourself.

Love much,
Beth Summers

{ Getting Started }

If the ideas in this book are a little out there for you, that's ok! I recognize that it's a totally different way of looking at, understanding and experiencing food. The preface is just my way of explaining my natural progression of how I've come to this conclusion, that all food is worthwhile because it's a symbol of how we see ourselves.

Food is a universal language, which is why it speaks to so many on various levels. For the most part, we've only approached food from a physical level. I'm suggesting we start looking at our food on a deeper level, to learn how to use it as a tool for self-reflection and a moderator in all things wellness.

I chose to divide this workbook into four different sections: body, mind, emotions and spirit. Each section consists of ten activities that help explore each level of health as it relates to food and self. Many of the challenges overlap, and even though one might be labeled as a spiritual activity, it absolutely has the potential to affect you emotionally, mentally, and/or physically. Because the truth is that each of these areas are interconnected and cannot be separated. We are the sum total of all that we experience.

We don't need any more books telling us what we should or shouldn't eat. This is definitely NOT a typical book about food. I do not intend to lecture anyone about the merits of one diet over the other, or one type of food over another. I'm simply inviting people to step outside the box and shift their food paradigm. So let's get started!

How it Works

This is an experiential workbook, an interactive food journal of sorts. Not one where you count your calories, but where you write down your thoughts, feelings and emotions as you finish each task. You'll be asked to complete assignments that may or may not make sense or even seem silly. And you'll be encouraged to face your fears head on.

Go through this workbook sequentially or randomly. However, I do recommend practicing for a full 40 days to receive the greatest benefits this workbook has to offer. Please know that you can also choose to take as much time as you'd like to accomplish each task. Whether that means working through one activity per week/month, or experiencing each assignment according to your own internal schedule, only moving on to the next challenge when you feel ready. The choice is yours!

I realize that many of these activities may be classified as a trigger. Many people, if not most, are dealing with some kind of addiction or trauma. I have personally learned the importance of boundaries and identifying what my triggers are in a way to create a safe environment for my healing. However, the longer I'm in the recovery process I've come to realize the importance of using triggers as tools for further healing. Instead of running away from a trigger, I now dig deep and try to learn from its presence.

This workbook admittedly provides what I like to call "trigger points" or in other words, learning opportunities. I have purposefully created some experiences with a potential trigger in mind. I've done this not because I'm a sadist, but because I believe in YOU and in your ability to break through the "terror barrier." You can do hard things, and these stumbling blocks before you are nothing more than steps that lead you onward and upward.

A final note about triggers. The word itself can be a trigger. I remember the first time I heard someone refer to a positive experience as a trigger, and it was completely mind blowing to me. For so long I thought triggers were something to be avoided because all triggers were negative. I've since learned that positive triggers certainly exist as well and are also beneficial to understand, validate and explore. Simply stated, a trigger is a cause to an effect. I advise you to discover what exactly it means for you and your learning path.

If at any time you feel uncomfortable with a specific task, you are more than welcome to skip it or choose another optional activity. It's your healing journey and I would love nothing more than for you to learn how to trust yourself. However, do ask yourself the five W's before opting out: who, what, when, where and why is this particular exercise difficult? Is it in your best interest at this exact moment to address these triggers or is it better to save them for another day? Only you can answer these questions and only you get to decide.

Speaking of questions, each assignment has a list of questions relating to the activity. Many of them are repetitive from one assignment to the next. They are simply prompts. You are encouraged to answer them, but I strongly recommend writing more than a short response. Hopefully they inspire some deeper reflection beyond "yes" or "no." Remember, this is a journal for your eyes only. Write a detailed account of your experience as a whole, using the questions as a guide. Their purpose is to get your juices flowing so that you can blast through any potential writer's block. Write whatever and however much you'd like (the more the better).

And finally, there is no right or wrong way because each person will respond differently — and that's ok. As it should be! In fact, if you do worry that you're somehow doing it wrong, explore that thought. Where did it come from, and why do you feel that way? Or on the flip side, if the experiment seems too simple, why do you think that is and what are you going to do about it?

Expand your comfort zone. If the task appears easy, then make it difficult. Try practicing the challenge multiple times throughout the day, with various foods/meals, in different settings with different company, etc. Every task is meant to help you interact with your food in a NEW way. Push yourself above and beyond your normal routine and learn more about something you're already familiar with.

When all is said and done, please know that there is support available as needed. I am here for you and will be more than happy to coach you one-on-one, get you in touch with a support group, or help you find professional counseling that is most conducive to your healing.

Why 40 Days

"You are what you eat." It's a rather common saying, and in my opinion quite cliché. In the yogic sciences there's a more accurate proverb: "Your habits define you."

One summer, I helped co-create a weekend event for women where I learned some powerful lessons. As I sat pondering on the flight home about everything that happened, I had a series of suggested food experiences pop into my head. Rather than analyze them, I started writing them down as fast as they came. I ended up with 40 different activities related to food! Now that's a significant number. You see, 40 is a sacred number. It represents a lot of different things to a lot of different people. For example, Yogi Bahjan believed that 40 days "will break any negative habits that block you from [expansion]."

While this book really isn't meant as a discourse on the merits of yoga, I find the parallels fascinating and worth exploring. It's interesting to note that there are other days of importance in addition to the initial 40 days. These include 90, 120 and 1,000 days. Each longer time period further breaks old harmful habits that no longer serve you and increases the resilience of newer habits that support your highest good.

As mentioned previously, you can choose to experience this workbook a day at a time with a new task per day for 40 days. Or maybe you'll decide to repeat the activities over and over, for 1,000 days total! You could also pick a single challenge and stick with it for 40 days or more. However you decide to go about it, I promise you will have a powerful and life changing experience if you allow your inner light to shine.

"EVERY SOUL [IS] PERFECT,
PURE AND DIVINE AT THE START.
THERE IS NOTHING TO REDEEM
OR PURIFY AT THE SOUL-LEVEL.
THE SOUL IS COMPLETE
AND BEAUTIFUL AS IT IS.
BUT LIFE IS BASED ON OUR HABITS.
OUR HABITS DEFINE US TO
OURSELVES AND TO OTHER PEOPLE.
BY OUR HABITS, WE LIVE IN PEACE
AND HAPPINESS. BY OUR HABITS,
WE CREATE MISERY AND PAIN.
WHEN WE CHANGE OUR HABITS,
EVERYTHING AROUND US
CAN CHANGE."
—3HO

Feast Journey 1

Through the power of our minds we can locate and then heal those deepest fears, lingering pains, and limiting beliefs. Before you begin on your food-related tasks, it's important to gauge where you are emotionally with regards to food. I invite you to complete the visualization and answer the questions below. When the 40 days are up, I'll ask you to do the guided meditation again to see how far you've come on your journey.

Included with this workbook is a link to a guided meditation to help facilitate an imagery journey from the comforts of your own home. Find a quiet and safe place before starting your session. Listen to the meditation and simply allow your thoughts and feelings to flow.

True Food: Feast Journey –
Banquet Hall Guided Meditation

https://www.youtube.com/watch?v=cdh3eNH spQc&feature=youtu.be

After you've completed the visualization exercise, answer the following questions:

- Did you find this exercise triggering?

- How did you feel about your relationship with food when you woke up?

- What conflicting emotions did you have (if any)?

> "What happens to us is not as important
> as the meaning we assign to it.
> Journaling helps sort this out."
> —Michael Hyatt

{ BODY }

Smell

There are so many food/diet fads nowadays. Gluten free, dairy free, paleo, vegan, flexitarian, clean eating, and the list goes on. Why is it that some diets seem to work for some and not for others? In my opinion and experience, it has everything to do with mindful eating. When someone becomes more aware of what they're eating and then do so intentionally, their body responds. But I believe there is a simpler way to eat mindfully that has less to do with what you're eating and more to do with how you're eating.

The easiest way to be mindful is to be present, and we do that by engaging all of our senses. Our body is such a gift! It is here to help us co-create with our soul a reality that serves our highest good. Being present allows us to connect with our inner self, which then allows us to connect with the world around us. And connecting with our food by smelling it is one of my favorite ways to develop a loving relationship with ourself.

Our sense of smell is directly tied to the limbic center in our brain, which helps process emotions. Have you ever walked past a rose bush or a plate of cookies only to be overwhelmed with the memory, and accompanying emotions, of your grandmother? Or maybe you catch a whiff of something less pleasant and it triggers an unkind thought, a traumatic reminder of darker days.

When we tune in to our senses and use them as an opportunity to further process any lingering or trapped emotions, we become more aware of our present moment.

Today, I want you to focus on your sense of smell whenever you encounter food. You can choose to smell each bite of a single meal, or take a quick whiff of every food item you come across throughout the day. As you do so, dig deep and see what comes up. Do not discount any memory, correlation, thought or feeling. Take note of everything that surfaces as you take the time to connect with your food.

JOURNAL PROMPTS

- What was your first thought when you were asked to smell your food?

- Did you find this exercise triggering? What conflicting emotions did you experience?

- Did you enjoy your time spent eating? Why do you think that is?

- Were you able to pick up the subtle qualities of individual food items? For example, the earthy scent of a pickled beet; or maybe the tang of the brine.

- If possible, invite someone to dine with you and practice this activity together. Compare and contrast the various scents with each other and discuss the similarities or differences you both experience.

"SMELL IS A POTENT WIZARD
THAT TRANSPORTS YOU
ACROSS THOUSANDS OF MILES
AND ALL THE YEARS
YOU HAVE LIVED."
—HELEN KELLER

Taste

I love to cook! It is one of my very favorite things to do. But following a recipe? Not so much. Cooking is a very intuitive process for me, and I taste as I go. In fact, as odd as it sounds, I can actually taste something without tasting it. So when my physical taste buds sync up with my imaginative taste buds, magic happens.

Unfortunately, there are times when I'm so distracted that I don't listen to either of my taste buds. I end up inhaling food rather than enjoying it, which leaves me feeling empty and unsatisfied. Our sense of taste is directly tied to our ability to create, which is why cooking can be such a joyful and fulfilling experience! Especially because taste goes hand in hand with smelling. Eating something just isn't the same when you have a stuffy nose! Why is that? Because we're unable to connect with our food, which further inhibits our ability to create a satisfying experience.

You might have already noticed a heightened sense of taste when practicing the smell experience. Focus more on tasting your food today, rather than smelling it. Really try to pick out individual flavors of each food item. If it tastes delicious, discover what it is that you enjoy so much about it.

Describe what it is you're tasting, going beyond "yummy" or "yucky" adjectives. Pretend you're a professional food taster and see if you can pick up on the subtle qualities of your dish. As you do so, take note of how you're feeling or what you're thinking. Share these physical and spiritual revelations with someone else, and then listen to their feelings and thoughts.

JOURNAL PROMPTS

- What was your first thought when you were asked to taste your food?

- Did you find this exercise triggering? What conflicting emotions did you experience?

- Did you enjoy your time spent eating? Why do you think that is?

- Do you feel inspired to do something fun or new? If so, what is it and why?

- Is it difficult sharing your discoveries, or does it make it more gratifying?

> *"The purpose of life is to live it,*
> *to taste experience to the utmost,*
> *to reach out eagerly and without fear*
> *for newer and richer experience."*
> *—Eleanor Roosevelt*

See

If the saying "seeing is believing" is true, then what is it that you see in the mirror? Also consider what you see in others. Do you only pay attention to their faults and weaknesses? How does it feel when you witness a child's first steps, a blooming rosebud, or a roaring waterfall? Our sense of sight helps shape the world around us, and it's also a good indicator of how we see ourselves.

My greatest mission in this life is to remind people of who they are, to act as a mirror of sorts so that they can learn to see their true reflections as valuable individuals. If you struggle to see your worth, please know you're not alone. Start small, and focus on the positive attributes that you do recognize. Notice your talents, look for the strengths in others, and try seeing the good in your food.

Your task is to really see your food. Be present before you bite; acknowledge the visual attributes of your meal. Does it look appetizing? Notice the colors, the way it's prepared, how it looks in different lighting, etc. I want you to embrace the blemishes you're sure to notice, and then look beyond its physical appearance. What do you see?

JOURNAL PROMPTS

- What was your first thought when you were asked to see your food?

- Did you find this exercise triggering? What conflicting emotions did you experience?

- Did you enjoy your time spent eating? Why do you think that is?

- Do you feel empowered to do something hard? If so, what is it and why?

> "We don't see things as they are,
> we see them as we are."
> —Anaïs Nin

Touch

Aw, touch. One of the five love languages and such an important sense that scientific research has shown how damaging it can be when touch is denied (Harlow's baby monkey study, newborn's need for skin-to-skin, etcetera). Touch allows us to connect with our outer world in a tangible way, as well as provide a palpable way to create our hopes and dreams. And in many ways, expressing our thoughts and feelings through touch takes a fair amount of courage.

Your assignment today is to feel your food. How does it feel in your hand as you hold it? Try stroking it with both sides of a single finger. How does it feel when you bring it to your lips? Experiment touching different kinds of food with different parts of your body and notice its texture, temperature, etc. As you take a bite, recognize how it feels in your mouth and notice any changes as you continue to chew before swallowing.

I realize that there is the potential for this activity to evoke sensual thoughts or feelings. But this experiment can also be done safely in public, with family and friends. It's really up to you in however you choose to experience your food. By now you're beginning to realize how each of your senses build on each other, and you find yourself moving from connection to creation to courage and now love. It's no wonder that by being presently engaged with the way our body works externally we are better able to discover the inner workings of our soul.

Journal Prompts

- What was your first thought when you were asked to touch your food?

- Did you find this exercise triggering? What conflicting emotions did you experience?

- Did you enjoy your time spent eating? Why do you think that is?

- Do you feel more in touch with your inner self?

- Do you feel more in touch with your external surroundings or relationships?

> "The greatest technology in the world hasn't replaced the ultimate relationship building tool between a customer and a business; the human touch."
> —Shep Hyken

Hear

Listening to our external surroundings as well as our internal settings, is key to learning and embodying truth. What we choose to hear helps shape our reality and the way we respond, or react, to those perceived truths. Taking the time to stop and listen requires a certain amount of self-discipline, as well. In this day and age, getting in touch with our sense of hearing is definitely a skill worth developing.

There are so many ways to experience our food when we listen to it. Today your task is to hear your food during every phase of usage. Carefully thunk it on the table and notice what sounds it makes. Bring it to your ear and flick it, listening to the sound vibrations emanating from it. As you prepare your meals in the kitchen, what does it sound like when you slice and dice? Relish in the sizzling resonance of cooking food. Have you ever noticed the quick "zip" of oven-cooked bacon, signaling it's done? Very different than the snap, crackle and pop of stove-top cooking. And last but certainly not least, how does it all sound when you start to chew?

It's important to notice the sounds of your eating environment. Graciously accept any praises, allow background noises to come and go, and tune in to what your body is telling you — it's time to listen.

Journal Prompts

- What was your first thought when you were asked to hear your food?

- Did you find this exercise triggering? What conflicting emotions did you experience?

- Did you enjoy your time spent eating? Why do you think that is?

- Do you feel more in touch with your inner truth?

- Have you recognized some falsehoods that are in need of addressing? If so, what is it and how will you change?

- Please list two truths and a lie that you've discovered through this process.

Adjust

By now we've experimented being present with our food by using all of our five senses. Hopefully you're beginning to feel more connected, creative, empowered, compassionate, and authentic with both yourself and others. Do you also feel more alive? I hope so.

Now we're going to switch gears a bit and remove one sense of your choosing while engaging the remaining four. See if you're able to pick up on something you might have otherwise missed. You could even turn it into a game! For example, blindfold a willing participant and hand them a specific food item. Have them describe it as they smell, taste, touch and listen. Take turns, asking questions and creating an open dialogue as you discuss their thoughts and feelings as well as your own.

Notice how your body acclimates to sensory deprivation and recognize the adjustments it makes. Some adaptations will be automatic, while others will require focus and determination. However you respond physically, pay attention to the more subtle responses happening from deeper within.

Journal Prompts

- What was your first thought when you were asked to complete this task?

- Did you find this exercise triggering? What conflicting emotions did you experience?

- Did you enjoy your time spent eating? Why do you think that is?

- Which particular sense did you choose to omit and why?

- When one sense was missing, were other senses heightened?

- Do you feel less in touch with your inner and outer world, or more so?

- How did it feel when you denied yourself experiencing food in a particular way? Where did you feel this new sensation?

> *"It is not love that should be depicted as blind, but self-love."*
> *–Voltaire*

Chew & Swallow

It's time to slow down. Your life might feel anything but slow, yet you have the power to set the pace if you choose. I believe our hunger cues are messages with the opportunity to pause and reconnect. If we can learn to engage with our food, as opposed to gulping it, we can learn to be present in life rather than consumed by it.

Your assignment is to be intentional about chewing and swallowing your food. Before taking a bite or sip, take five deep relaxing breaths, in through the nose and out through the mouth. As you chew, do so slowly and thoroughly. Try counting how many times your jaw moves up and down, or set a timer to see how long it takes, until the food is completely masticated. Notice your thoughts as you chew. Do they wander distractedly, or are you focused on processing your food? Does the flavor change as the texture morphs from solid to liquid (the ideal swallowing state)? Toward the end of your meal, do you find yourself more satiated than usual?

When drinking, take time to let your beverage intermingle with your saliva. If your water is ice-cold, let it sit in your mouth until it reaches body temperature before swallowing. Can you tell a difference in the consistency? How does your throat feel as you swallow? Imagine following your meal along its digestive journey, starting with the first taste and ending with the final destination of elimination. Visualize your body efficiently absorbing everything it needs and easily excreting everything it doesn't.

JOURNAL PROMPTS

- What was your first thought when you were asked to slowly chew/swallow your food and drinks?

- Did you find this exercise triggering? What conflicting emotions did you experience?

- Did you enjoy your time spent eating? Why do you think that is?

- Was it difficult to slow down? If so, why?

- Do you feel more relaxed? More satisfied?

Last Bite

I know a few people, myself included, who really struggle with leaving their plate empty. It triggers a scarcity mindset, a false belief that there isn't enough or that they're unsafe and food provides a type of sanctuary. Some were also raised to clean every last crumb from their plates and consequently as adults have a hard time not finishing everything on their plate out of fear of being in trouble or seeming ungrateful. Even though logically we can tell ourselves that there is enough food, that we are safe and that we can regulate our own satiety free from judgment, there is an emotional disconnect. And that is what we are trying to explore and address in this exercise.

Just for today, I want you to save a last bite of everything on your plate. You can then choose to throw it away, or savor each individual bite using all of your senses. Another option is to create the perfect last bite. I do this all the time and was surprised that most people don't. When I take my first bite I'm calculating what my last bite is going to look like. Eating a sandwich, for example, becomes a work of art and my poor husband has learned to NEVER take a bite from my plate unless asking first. Generally, I save the perfect little bite of just about everything in order to create the ultimate perfect big bite of everything.

Savor that last bite with everything you've got and thoroughly enjoy the process, as well as the conclusion. Sometimes, that perfect last bite comes earlier than originally planned. Practice letting go of the remaining food on your plate, preferably ending on a richly satisfying morsel than an unsatisfyingly empty one.

JOURNAL PROMPTS

- What was your first thought when you were asked to save or leave your food?

- Which option did you choose and why?

- Did you find this exercise triggering? What conflicting emotions did you experience?

- Did you enjoy your time spent eating? Why do you think that is?

- How did you feel about your meal as a whole?

- Was it difficult to leave food on your plate? This question applies to either option, as you temporarily leave bites alone in preparation for the final bite vs. permanently leaving remaining bites alone to be thrown out.

> "Develop an appreciation for the present moment. Seize every second of your life and savor it."
> –Dr. Wayne Dyer

Take a Pic

Thanks to social media, "Food Porn" is everywhere! Pinterest, Instagram and Facebook are prime examples. And it seems like any mommy blogger with a nice camera is the next Martha Stewart. Most people buy recipe books and watch food shows because of the attractive display of pretty food. Commercials do their darndest to lure us to restaurants we might have otherwise avoided. Before you know it, we've wasted hours looking at food without ever eating it.

And now it's your turn to play paparazzi! For today's task, take pictures of your food not for other people's eyes but for yours. Take the time to capture the essence of a meal, snack, or anything that passes your lips. This can be literal or figurative. Get creative and try your best to honor the truest representation of what you're eating before, during and after.

> "To me, photography is an art of observation. It's about finding something interesting in an ordinary place... I've found it has little to do with the things you see and everything to do with the way you see them."
> —Elliott Erwitt

JOURNAL PROMPTS

- What was your first thought when you were asked to photograph your food?

- Did you find this exercise triggering? What conflicting emotions did you experience?

- Did you enjoy your time spent eating? Why do you think that is?

- How did you feel about your meal as a whole?

> "Taking pictures is savoring life intensely,
> every hundredth of a second."
> —Marc Riboud

Picnic

Life's no picnic, right? It's hard! But it doesn't have to be...

When's the last time you went on a picnic? Well now's your chance! You can go solo, with a friend, or make it a family outing. Try somewhere new to explore, whether it's an exotic location or rediscovering your backyard. Turn it into a memorable event by hanging Christmas lights, spreading out a cozy quilt, and creating a special playlist just for the occasion.

And don't forget the most important part: food! It can be simple, playful finger food or an elaborate fancy three-course meal. Consider moving the dinner table outside and serving supper al fresco style. Print out a fun menu that briefly describes your chosen meal items, including even mundane items such as condiments or beverages.

Whether you choose to enjoy a sunny brunch or brave a snack in the middle of a thunderstorm, try experiencing your food in a completely different environment than you're used to. There are so many missed dining opportunities! Now is the time to take a bite out of life and relish each moment.

JOURNAL PROMPTS

- What was your first thought when you were asked to plan a picnic?

- Did you find this exercise triggering? What conflicting emotions did you experience?

- Did you enjoy your time spent planning?

- Was it difficult to think about your food extravagantly? If so, why?

- How did you feel about food before, during, and after the picnic?

> *"There are few things so pleasant as a picnic eaten in perfect comfort."*
> *—W. Somerset Maugham*

{ MIND }

Roots

Food plays a huge role in cultures around the world and in family traditions. As we've experienced our food through our physical senses, a lot of our memories and beliefs around food can be traced back to how we were raised. This is true for both positive and negative experiences. In order to discover who we are and where we're going, it helps to see where we come from.

For example, even though I don't look it I come from an Italian background on my Dad's side. I grew up making homemade raviolis for Christmas Dinner. As for my maternal grandmother, I never knew her. But I do have memories that my mother has passed down about her mother's cooking, and I treasure her grandmother's recipe for ginger molasses cookies.

Rediscover food by filling out the family tree provided with recipes and traditions, or memories, beliefs, etc. Dig deep as you unearth just how far the apple falls from the tree.

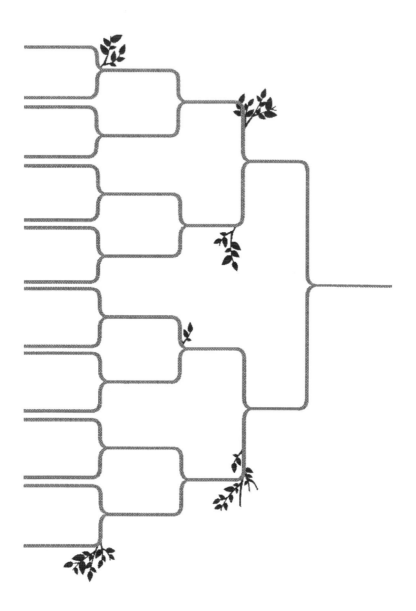

JOURNAL PROMPTS

- What was your first thought when you were asked to catalogue, or index, your food?

- Did you find this exercise triggering? What conflicting emotions did you experience?

- Did you enjoy your time reminiscing? Why or why not?

- Where did your love for, or hate of, food come from?

- How do the details of your lineage, or roots, behind family favorites and food traditions affect you now?

Meet & Greet

There is a face behind every food, and eating can be a personal experience if we allow it. Think of all the people who were involved in bringing a meal to your table. If possible, visit the local Farmer's Market and introduce yourself to every vendor. Shake hands with them, meet their eyes with yours and get to know them. Ask them how they feel about their products. What sets them apart from anyone else? How long have they been in their particular business? Recognize that they are passionate about what they're offering at their booth and that they're essentially sharing a part of themselves with you. Be receptive to their message and honor your time together.

You may also wish to do this at your nearby grocery store. Thank the store clerks by name. Notice the men and women behind the counters and strike up a conversation with them. It can be something as benign as talking about the flowers or cheese on display, or you could choose to volunteer something vulnerable about yourself to these otherwise strangers. Maybe you've had a bad day, but the sample lady helped lessen your load with a single smile. Let her know how she has served you, and perhaps you could think of a way to serve her in return the next time you meet.

As you mix and mingle with those who interact with your food, open yourself up to the possibility of developing new relationships. Strangers become acquaintances with exciting opportunities for further bonding. After all, you both have a mutual friend: food.

> *"Fear makes strangers of people who would be friends."*
> *—Shirley MacLaine*

JOURNAL PROMPTS

- What was your first thought when you were asked to meet your food?

- Did you find this exercise triggering? What conflicting emotions did you experience?

- Did you enjoy your time spent greeting/visiting and why?

- Was it difficult to think about your food conversationally? If so, why?

- How did you feel about food before, during, and after the trip?

- Was it easier or harder to enjoy eating when you knew where it came from and what went into it? Are you looking forward to the next time you eat?

"SUCCESS OCCURS
WHEN STRANGERS
BECOME FRIENDS."
–JOHN WILKES

Speak Kindly

I'm going to assume that we've all heard about studies where scientists talked to plants, with surprising results. The plants thrived! Another favorite experiment of mine is the love/hate rice. This one fascinates me and I personally know friends who have used this to teach their children the importance of using nice words and thinking kind thoughts. In case you have no idea what I'm talking about, let me fill you in:

Cook up a batch of rice. Divide it in half and place it in two separate jars. Identify one as the love rice and the other as the hate rice. For the next few days, praise your love rice with compliments and adoration while saying and thinking horrible things to the hate rice. Observe any changes. By the end of the week, one jar is full of beautiful fluffy rice and the other contains nasty mush. Guess which jar is which.

Now, let's take this a step further. Imagine eating those jars of rice. I've never once seen anyone eat either servings of rice at the end of the home rice experiment. Ever. Because, gross. But that's essentially what we're doing every day! Not only do our words affect us and others, it affects our food. The very stuff we're eating is full of all those positive or negative statements. It may not sit on the counter for a week, yet the damage has already been done.

Today is different. Because today you're going to speak loving, kind words to everything that even remotely resembles food. This includes fresh fruit, raw vegetables, processed junk and beverages of all kinds. Take it a step further by assigning an uplifting phrase to each bite you take and imagine filling your body with positivity.

Journal Prompts

- What was your first thought when you were asked to complete this task?

- Did you find this exercise triggering? Any conflicting emotions?

- Did you enjoy your time spent eating? Why do you think that is?

- How did it feel eating kindness? Were you more satiated than normal?

> "Kind words are a creative force,
> a power that concurs in the building
> up of all that is good, and energy
> that showers blessings upon the world."
> —Lawrence G. Lovasik

Sweet Dreams

All right, brace yourself. I want you to sleep with your food. It could be anything: an apple, granola bar, lollipop, whatever comes to mind! Don't just set it on your nightstand; I want you to cuddle with it. Let it rest on your pillow and under your sheets with you. Imagine it as a slumber party and have fun!

I know, I know. At first it sounds totally bogus! But if you think about it, we bring food to bed ALL the time. An indulgent breakfast in bed, fancy little mints on our hotel pillows, erotic whipped cream or sensual chocolate sauce with that special someone, etc. On the flip side, I once knew a little boy who would hoard his food under his bed due to an insecure environment at home. Food was his special safety net.

The idea here is to spend time with your food in what at first seems an unconventional way, and then notice what comes up for you. Food can be special all the time! We don't need an excuse to enjoy it.

JOURNAL PROMPTS

- What was your first thought when you were asked to sleep with your food?

- Did you find this exercise triggering?

- Did you sleep well, or poorly? Why do you think that is?

- How did you feel about your food item when you woke up?

- If you chose to eat your food, what conflicting emotions did you experience (if any)?

- If you chose to throw away your food, what conflicting emotions did you have?

- How would you feel if you were to eat it now? Could you eat it with gratitude, knowing that it's served its purpose?

> "Man cannot long survive without air, water, and sleep. Next in importance comes food. And close on its heels, solitude."
> –Thomas Szasz

Visualize

Many nowadays have food intolerances or allergies. There's a mile long list of things to avoid: gluten, dairy, MSG, hydrogenated oils, food dye, etc. It's no wonder that the more we've focused on what to avoid the more we've created a hostile world of food. It's time to reverse the tide and stop thinking of the things we don't want and start focusing on the things we do want.

Create a vision board of foods you'd like to enjoy this year. Maybe it could be pictures of a particular five star restaurant, or a certain recipe you'd like to try. If you do suffer from allergies or intolerances, try finding images that represent comfort and wellness, taking care to place them alongside potential trigger foods.

Imagine yourself enjoying food again. What does it look like? How does it feel? Capture those thoughts and emotions with magazine clippings, printed memes or scribbled quotes. Get creative and have a good time visualizing the possibilities!

JOURNAL PROMPTS

- What was your first thought when you were asked to visualize your food?

- Did you find this exercise triggering? What conflicting emotions did you experience?

- Did you enjoy your time spent dreaming and why?

- Was it difficult to think about food in a creative, proactive way? If so, why?

- How did you feel about your food before, during, and after the experience?

- Was it easier or harder to enjoy eating foods you envisioned? Are you looking forward to the next time you eat?

Plan

I love meal planning! But then again, I'm a list-maker (not to be confused with a list-follower). I've been consistently planning meals for our family for years, and I sometimes forget how daunting it can seem for others. So I'm going to teach you how:

1. List as many of your favorite meals off the top of your head. Now is not the time to worry about "off limit foods." Simply brainstorm, including your family and friends in the process.

2. Go through cookbooks and websites to help jog your memory and/or come up with meals you'd like to try.

3. Organize your meals into seven categories. For example: Mexican, Italian, Vegetarian, Soups, Salads, etc.

4. Decide on your food-related goals: Eat fish once a week, have a leftovers night, incorporate more meatless meals, take-out, etc.

5. Create theme nights based off of steps 3 and 4. Assign each day of the week with a type of meal to plan around. Use silly names to make it fun, exciting, and easy to remember: Mexican Monday, Oriental Tuesday, Twisted Wednesday (recycled leftovers), Authentic Thursday, TGIFriday, Super Simple Saturday, Special Sunday.

6. Refer back to your list of meals from steps 1 and 2. Start plugging meal ideas into your theme nights, while keeping your goals in mind: Fish once a week results in fish tacos for Mexican Monday one week, and shrimp scampi for Authentic Thursday the following week.

7. Make sure to schedule date nights and intersperse difficult/experimental meals with fast/easy meals. Save the fancy stuff for the weekends when you have more time. Make new meals out of old ones (leftovers), so you're left with minimal prep work while diversifying your meals: Leftover pot roast from Sunday will make for a great beef stew on Wednesday.

8. Start with scheduling 1-2 weeks at a time. Gradually build up to a month's worth of meals, then four months. Repeat your rotation of meals every three months, and before you know it you'll have a year's worth of meals planned!

9. Print out your year's worth of meals and file away in a binder. Include a calendar for each month, with its corresponding recipes and shopping lists for future use. Keep pages in clear sheet protectors to protect them from spills and splatters. If you'd rather have your meal plan in a digital format, look into ZipList or RecipeBox. There are a lot of websites and apps available that help keep your meals organized, making it readily accessible if you keep a smart phone or tablet with you.

To ward off the dreaded "What's for breakfast/lunch/dinner?" question(s), print out a weekly calendar and display it on the fridge. That way everyone knows what they're eating and when they're eating it. Make it easy: Keep breakfasts, lunches and snacks simple so you're not burned out come dinner time. Feel free to use the weekly calendar below as a guide to help you create your own schedule.

	MON	TUES	WED	THURS	FRI	SAT	SUN
B	oatmeal	egg & ham scramble	rice & raisin porridge	fried eggs w/ bacon	granola	pancakes & eggs	pancake parfait
L	turkey roll-ups w/ olives	PB&J sand-wich w/ apples	turkey roll-ups w/ olives	PB&J sand-wich w/ apples	turkey roll-ups w/ olives	leftovers/ snacks	leftovers/ snacks
D	Mexican	Oriental	Twisted (leftovers)	Authentic	TGIF	Date Night (cereal)	Dad's choice

Snack Ideas:
1. granola bar
2. popcorn
3. trail mix
4. crackers w/ hummus
5. fresh fruit/veggies
6. smoothie/green drink

Now let's stop and think for a minute. I've essentially taught you how to plan your meals, on the off chance you didn't know how. Armed with this knowledge, how likely are you to actually plan your meals? There are several apps, programs, websites and Pinterest boards that offer meal planning services and ideas. How interesting that meal prep continues to be a source of frustration and fear! Why is that?

Maybe it seems like a huge waste of time, and there are plenty of other things you'd rather be doing. Or perhaps you feel like no matter what you plan or cook for dinner, it goes unappreciated. You may feel burnt out and stretched thin, naturally resenting adding more service to your already full plate. Consider what meal planning means to you and see if you can shift your perception into something that serves you.

JOURNAL PROMPTS

- What was your first thought when you were asked to plan out your food?

- Did you find this exercise triggering? What conflicting emotions did you experience?

- Did you enjoy your time spent researching/planning and why?

- Was it difficult to think about your food proactively? If so, why?

- How did you feel about your meals before, during, and after planning?

- Was it easier or harder to enjoy eating when you already knew what you were going to eat? Did you look forward to meal time?

- Optional: Continue to journal about your meals, noticing what emotions arise as you approach and complete each one. Do it for at least a day.

Shop

Time to shift our paradigm, again! Let's spend some time focusing on nutrient dense versus empty calories. We've done a great job as a society vilifying processed food. But what have we done to our health food? We've reduced it to physical limitations, and we now find ourselves consuming physically rich yet spiritually empty food. What about those who don't have access to the best food possible? Are they doomed?

Let's say the world is about to end and we head to the hills to live in tents. Well, we won't have access to the "best" food possible. What then? Or think about the Israelites who lived off of manna for so long — not your most varied diet, yet they survived for years! I really do believe that our bodies are capable of pulling what they need from their food source, especially if done mindfully. Unfortunately, starvation and food deficiencies are real. However, it is possible to hold space for our fallen food, so that its inner light resonates with and nourishes our inner light.

For this exercise I want you to come up with a shopping list. Obviously, include the ingredients you'll need for your upcoming weekly meals (refer to meal plan). Then, decide how often you want to go to the grocery store. I know some prefer to make as few trips as possible and do it all in one fell swoop, while others like to shop as often as once a day. You could even call your local grocer about their delivery services, or experiment purchasing groceries online! Whichever one you're used to doing, try the other approach and shake things up a bit by expanding your comfort zone.

Next, as you purchase your food I want you to buy something fun or special just for you. Maybe it's a sweet treat or a fancy cheese. You can choose to list this item on your premeditated shopping list or you can spontaneously throw it in your cart when you get there and something speaks to you. Also, buy something you normally wouldn't. For example, if you're used to buying organic then buy something nonorganic and vice versa. Especially if you've always looked down your nose on those who purchase otherwise.

Lastly, stay in the present moment as your shopping trip comes to a close. Whether it's interacting with the cashier as you write out a check or swiping your credit card at the self-checkout stand. Try something different and notice how you feel as you do so.

JOURNAL PROMPTS

- What was your first thought when you were asked to buy your food?

- Did you find this exercise triggering? What conflicting emotions did you experience?

- Did you enjoy your time spent shopping and why?

- How did you feel about your meals before, during, and after your purchase?

"IF YOU CAN'T FEED
A HUNDRED PEOPLE,
THEN FEED JUST ONE."
—MOTHER TERESA

Tourist

Eating becomes personal if, or when, we want it to. But how often is eating an act of the heart? Whenever you feel conflicted about your food choices or eating habits, give yourself a few minutes to connect with your breath and then act with your full heart. As you do so, realize that you have the potential to extend that connection outward.

Visit a nearby farm, u-pick patch or food factory. Go on a tour of the facilities and get some hands on experience if possible. Make sure to take lots of pictures and ask as many questions as you possibly can! What does a normal schedule look like for them? How do they handle sick animals, blighted crops or bruised goods? What is the process involved with quality control, and what happens to the discarded items? Why do they do what they do? You can even ask them how much it all costs and what their profit margins are. Sign up for their newsletter so you can stay in touch. And finally, ask for their mailing address and send a thank you letter at your earliest convenience.

Find out as much as you can while shadowing the people behind your food. Try to imagine what it would be like if the roles were reversed. No matter who you are or what you do, everyone and everything relies on food. In all reality, eating is rarely an isolated act if we take the time to realize how connected we truly are.

JOURNAL PROMPTS

- What was your first thought when you were asked to tour your food?

- Did you find this exercise triggering? What conflicting emotions did you experience?

- Did you enjoy your time spent researching/visiting and why?

- Was it difficult to think about your food adventurously? If so, why?

- How did you feel about food before, during, and after the trip?

- Was it easier or harder to enjoy eating when you knew where it came from and what went into it? Are you looking forward to the next time you eat?

> "One's destination is never a place,
> but a new way of seeing things."
> —Henry Miller

Volunteer

One of the best ways to get to know yourself better is to get outside of yourself and observe. Witness the relationship others have with their food and recognize what you have in common. Notice that by observing, you're actually attending to the needs we all share.

Go to a soup kitchen and get to work. Help prepare and serve the meal, intermingling with other volunteers as well as the benefactors. As you do so, take in your surroundings. Be as mindful and present as you can, engaging all your senses and connecting with those you interact with. Try to put yourself in their shoes. Why did this woman come to help today? And why is that man here to eat today? Ask questions, speak kindly when spoken to and if possible share a meal with someone at the venue.

When it is time to clean up, ponder upon the entire experience from start to finish. Witness the food in the trash, on the floor, in the sink, etc. Mentally praise it for a job well done. This food held sacred space for a tiny moment, by allowing service to be rendered and received. Thank it for the wonderful, humble teacher that it is.

JOURNAL PROMPTS

- What was your first thought when you were asked to volunteer with food?

- Did you find this exercise triggering? What conflicting emotions did you experience?

- Did you enjoy your time spent interacting and why?

- Was it difficult to think about your food as a gift? If so, why?

- How did you feel about food before, during, and after the experience?

- Was it easier or harder to enjoy eating when you knew it would be appreciated by someone, somewhere? Are you looking forward to the next time you eat?

> "If you knew what I know about the power of giving, you would not let a single meal pass without sharing it in some way."
> —Buddha

Homeless

Everyone matters, regardless of their fortunate circumstances, or the lack thereof. And everyone is hungry. Not just physically starving, but spiritually as well. Unfortunately, not everyone has a roof over their head. But we all have one thing in common: a human body that houses a spirit.

Put together a few care packages to have on hand in your car to pass out to those in need. Include an unopened water bottle, granola bars and other nonperishable food items. Consider inserting a small gift card to a nearby fast food restaurant. As you create these kits, imagine filling each item with love and well wishes before sealing them with warm intentions.

The next time you pass by someone on the street, drive to the nearest grocery store and grab something from the deli. Return and personally hand deliver your food offering to them. Another option is to invite them to join your for breakfast or dinner. Let them order whatever they want, or take them to an all-you-can-eat buffet. Watch how they eat. Ask them what their favorite food is and why.

If any of these challenges are uncomfortable, ask yourself why that is and what you need to feel safe. Obviously, it is important that you are free from danger. I recommend attempting this task with someone else present. It could be a potentially powerful teaching lesson for not only yourself but also your children.

However, if danger is likely or if it is illegal to aid panhandlers, then please consider donating to a homeless shelter. Find out how they operate and ask what you can do to help.

As you look for ways to aid those less privileged than you, notice how full you feel. Satiety can be found outside the kitchen in life experiences that nourish both the giver and receiver. We might not be in a position to build a home, but we can feed a hungry soul.

JOURNAL PROMPTS

- What was your first thought when you were asked to donate your food?

- Did you find this exercise triggering? What conflicting emotions did you experience?

- Did you enjoy your time spent interacting and why?

- Was it difficult to think about your food as a gift? If so, why?

- How did you feel about food before, during, and after the experience?

- Was it easier or harder to enjoy eating when you knew it would be appreciated by someone, somewhere? Are you looking forward to the next time you eat?

{ EMOTIONS }

Newborn

Once upon a time, there was a little girl with big dreams and loving parents who wanted what was best for her. These parents also had loving parents, the loving grandparents of said girl. In this loving family, food was a tool. Something to be researched, studied, tested and evaluated. Food was believed to heal. Food was also believed to cause weight. Over the years, she came to fear and revere her food.

Nowadays, there's a word for it: orthorexia. This girl now understands that it's something she inherited and learned, both formally and informally. She has since discovered how damaging those feelings of "not enough" have been to her body, and spirit. And she's realized that it was her love of food and her fascination with the human body that ultimately saved her from losing herself completely.

That girl is me. I've found myself, my True Self, and every day I discover new ways to honor my body. Food is not the enemy. It's my best friend that helps me dig a little deeper. It reflects my emotions, both negative and positive, back to me for further processing. Because when I allow food to facilitate the healing process, it becomes a powerful tool to reconnect with myself and the world I was born into.

Now is your chance at rebirth. Pull out that list of baby names and head to the fridge or pantry to pick out your bundle of joy! Pretend you're back in home economics, but instead of toting a baby doll, you'll be carrying around a food item with you all day today. It can be anything from a bag of sugar to an apple. Carefully draw a face on it, add hair, accessories, whatever endears you to your food baby. Interact with it often, calling it by name and lovingly cooing at it. Take care of it just as you would a newborn infant.

When the day is over, sing your food a lullaby and give it a kiss before returning it to its resting place. Breathe easy knowing you've done your best. Tomorrow brings a new day; a chance at a new beginning.

Journal Prompts

- What was your first thought when you were asked to baby your food?

- Did you find this exercise triggering?

- Did you enjoy your time with your food? Why do you think that is?

- How did you feel about your food item at the end of the day?

- If you chose to eat your food, what conflicting emotions did you experience?

- As you babied your food, did you find yourself worth babying?

"IN GIVING BIRTH
TO OUR BABIES,
WE MAY FIND THAT
WE GIVE BIRTH
TO NEW POSSIBILITIES
WITHIN OURSELVES."
– MYLA & JON KABAT-ZINN

First Foods

Food is one of our basic human needs, from day one. What a baby eats is a large, and hot, topic of discussion. From the moment a woman conceives, she's inundated with the proper feeding and care of an infant. Breast is best! But, what if it isn't? Before a baby is even born, the new mother faces enormous pressure surrounding what and how to feed her precious bundle of joy. Sometimes those late night feedings provide tender moments of connection between mom and babe. And at other times, nursing turns into a power struggle with tears from both sides. If parents choose to bottle-feed, they face shame and disappointment of their peers, families, and even caregivers.

When it's finally time to introduce new foods, the decision between breast versus bottle now expands to an even longer list of do's and don'ts. More tears. And years of potential food fights with picky eaters. Is it any wonder why so many of us struggle with food into adulthood?

Bust out the bibs, because you're going to rediscover food as if it were the first time! If you're feeling brave and you have access to breastmilk, try it. Remember, chances are it isn't your first time. Or then again, maybe it is. Go to the store and buy an assortment of baby food to sample. You could also puree your own food at home. Eat with your hands, using your fingers like pincers and taking little bites at a time. Be messy. Don't worry about getting food on your face, in your hair or on the floor. Get in touch with your inner child; baby yourself and be the parent YOU need today.

Journal Prompts

- What was your first thought when you were asked to rediscover food?

- Did you find this exercise triggering?

- Did you enjoy your time with your food? Why do you think that is?

- What foods did you try and why?

- How did you feel about your food items before, during, and after the exercise?

- After sampling your first few bites, you may choose to throw it away or eat the rest of it. What conflicting emotions did you experience with your choice?

> *"First we eat. Then we do everything else."*
> *—M.F.K. Fisher*

Playtime

Let's stop fighting with our food and start playing with it! I firmly believe in child-led learning, and one of the best ways to learn is through play. Unfortunately, many of us have spent the majority of our lives learning in a very structured way. We're told to sit still, listen intently, and do as we're instructed. We learn to mistrust our natural curiosity, and instead wait for authoritative instruction. Eat this, not that.

When's the last time you listened to your inner gut wisdom? It's time to silence the outer critics and make inspired food choices again. Your eating habits don't have to be so controlled. Maybe it feels unsafe being out of control, and so you doubt your ability to make wise decisions. But you can. I believe in you.

Food connects us to our bodies, our mortal experience here on Mother Earth, and allows us to create a foundation for our spiritual selves. I invite you to shift from cautious eating into intuitive eating. So get in touch with your inner child and let loose! Eat with your hands and get creative. Stack your breakfast cereals, paint with your sauces, throw your rolls, etc.

This is especially fun in a group, but it can also be deeply rewarding when done on your own. Discover what you like, or what you don't like. Have fun getting to know your food! You might just start to understand yourself better, too.

Journal Prompts

- What was your first thought when you were asked to play with your food?

- Did you find this exercise triggering?

- Was it difficult to let yourself go? Did you feel out of control, or free?

- If you chose to eat your food, what conflicting emotions did you experience (if any)?

- Did you enjoy your time spent eating? Why do you think that is?

Craft Project

One of the greatest truths I've learned about myself is that I am creative. I love to sew, crochet, scrapbook, etc. But creativity is much more than crafting. When money is tight, I find a way to make it work. Decorating my house and keeping it tidy is extremely rewarding for me. Meal planning, recipe tweaking, and food coaching is obviously something I'm passionate about. What's your craft of choice?

Everyone has the power to create. If our ability to create is stifled then we feel like we've lost our ability to choose, and choice plays a pivotal role in creating our reality. We may feel out of control and disconnected; life becomes meaningless as we question our very existence. By re-engaging with our senses, we bring ourselves back to the present moment where we can connect and create enriching relationships of all kinds, on all levels. We remember who we are, why we're here and where we're going.

As you take some time to figure out exactly how you express creativity, hop on Pinterest to get those innovative juices flowing! Find a quirky food craft. You know, like the ones they come up with for preschool. Making a necklace out of finger foods is always a classic! Feel free to use your imagination and come up with something on your own. Let your inner inventor and hidden artist shine by creating a foodie masterpiece! Get the whole family to participate, especially involving little kids. You could probably learn a lesson or two from them.

Journal Prompts

- What was your first thought when you were asked to craft your food?

- Did you find this exercise triggering? What conflicting emotions did you experience?

- Did you enjoy your time spent creating and why?

- Was it difficult to think about your food artistically? If so, why?

- How did you feel about your food item when you crafting?

Show & Tell

What is a food you just can't say no to? A batch of cookies? Maybe some homemade bread. For me, it's chips. We all have those foods that tug at us.

For this task, make (or buy) something that has always had a hold on you, something you don't dare have around for fear of eating it all by yourself. Let it sit on your counter in plain sight and then call one or more friends. Invite them over to enjoy this food with you and share with them your love of this particular dish. Tell them what it is you love about it and why. Be very specific. Perhaps it's a childhood favorite, or something that excites all of your senses. Be vulnerable and share with them how you feel when you eat it.

You could even make a night of this, having everyone bring their favorite things. Anything goes, except for shaming. Expressing fears and digging deep together is encouraged, but absolutely no shaming language is allowed. There is no humiliation here, only love and support.

When the event is through, you have the option of either sending leftovers home with everyone or throwing it all away. You have filled yourself in a way this particular food item hasn't been able to in the past. Realize that it no longer controls you, and it is now safe to let it go. It's almost like saying goodbye to a dear friend, knowing that you'll meet again and enjoy your time together without being held hostage.

Journal Prompts

- What was your first thought when you were asked to share your food?

- Did you find this exercise triggering? What conflicting emotions did you experience?

- Did you enjoy your time spent eating? Why do you think that is?

- Was it difficult being vulnerable and transparent with others? If so, why?

- Do you feel more relaxed around your trigger food? More satisfied?

> "When you stand and share your story in an empowering way, your story will heal you and your story will heal somebody else."
> –Iyanla Vanzant

Dine In

I love when my husband prepares breakfast, lunch or dinner! Not only because it means I get a reprieve from cooking, but also because it's so fun watching him have fun cooking. And I swear that sandwiches taste better when he makes them.

Have someone cook for you, and just observe. The other option is to cook for someone else and have them watch you. The trick here is to refrain from any conversation. Tune in to your food as you prepare it, and imagine filling it with love and well wishes for the person witnessing you. Be present with the whole process, using your senses to connect with your food in preparation for connecting with your guest.

As the observer, pretend you're watching a commercial or cooking show. Notice how the cook interacts with their food. Watch their body language, the expressions on their face as they prepare the meal before you. While you may not verbally express your thoughts at this time, you are encouraged to send the chef positive thoughts. Mentally let them know how much you enjoy just being in their presence.

Sit down together and eat the freshly prepared meal. You may now engage in an open dialogue of what you experienced as both an observer and a presenter. Express your feelings for the food you're eating as well as each other. Thank them, and the meal, for providing you with this opportunity.

JOURNAL PROMPTS

- What was your first thought when you were asked to observe/present?

- Which option did you choose and why?

- Did you find this exercise triggering? What conflicting emotions did you experience?

- Did you enjoy your time spent eating? Why do you think that is?

- If you were the presenter, did you enjoy your time spent cooking and why?

- If you were the observer, did you enjoy your time spent witnessing and why?

- How did you feel about your meal as a whole?

- Was it difficult not speaking? What did you learn about differing perceptions?

> "A recipe has no soul, you as the
> cook must bring soul to the recipe."
> - Thomas Keller

Dine Out

Eating out is one of my favorite activities. Don't get me wrong, I love cooking. And eating. But there's something fun, even a little adventurous, about eating something I didn't make. A chance to put myself in someone else's shoes, and try to experience the food from their perspective in conjunction with my own. By appreciating the relationship others have with their food, it allows me an opportunity to connect with them in a uniquely intimate way, and develop a relationship with them personally.

There are so many different ways to enjoy dining out. Try something new, whether it's a different restaurant, a different appetizer or dessert, maybe even bring along a different dining guest. The next time you eat out, go a little outside of your comfort zone: order the most expensive item on the menu, or let someone else order for you. If you're dining alone, you can even let the waiter choose your next meal!

Money tight? Strict budget? I hear ya! Try thinking outside of the box, though. If your first thought is "I can't afford to eat out" then explore that a bit. What can you do to modify this assignment to make it work for you? It might require some research, coupon clipping, signing up for newsletters or membership clubs from restaurants, etc. Heck, even splitting a hot dog from Costco would count. Learn to let go of control and free yourself from self-perceived limitations.

Journal Prompts

- What was your first thought when you were asked to try something new?

- Which option did you choose and why?

- Did you find this exercise triggering? What conflicting emotions did you experience?

- Did you enjoy your time spent eating? Why do you think that is?

- How did you feel about your meal as a whole?

- Was it difficult to let go of control? What did you learn about differing perceptions?

Buffet Bar

There is power in choice. The truth is, food can be both good AND bad for you. Instead of forcing yourself into a false dichotomy, which creates internal conflict and the inability to make a decision, just sit with the two conflicting truths and allow yourself to validate both sides. For example, I love my children AND they drive me crazy. I do myself, and my children, a disservice when I believe that I am only capable of loving them OR of being inconvenienced by them. If I choose one truth over the other, I negate the other truth and create a falsehood in its place. "I love my children BUT they drive me crazy" makes me doubt my ability to be a good mother, because if I really loved my children then they wouldn't drive me crazy, right? Do you see how crazy-making that line of thinking is?

The same principle applies to food. You know yourself best, and so if a piece of cake is a trigger food for you and you're unable to keep yourself from eating the entire cake, then give yourself a little grace. That cake is not bad, it's deliciously tempting AND it's beautifully decorated AND it represents a deeper need to feel loved. All of these truths are valid, and you get to choose which truth to move forward with. Do not give away your power to the various stores, brands, magazines, etc. Their claims are less important than your beliefs, because you can choose to appreciate the beauty in the cake without eating it while simultaneously reaching out for support. You can also choose to take a bite, enjoy every second of it, and decide that your appreciation is complete and the rest of the cake no longer has a hold on you. Your food, your choice.

Today's task is to choose an assortment of delicacies and host your own taste-testing party! Buy different kind of chocolates, cookies and candies. Or go the savory route with various cheeses, crackers, meats, etc. Fun flavored beverages are also exciting to explore. Whichever option you choose, notice what emotions surface. Recognize what you're naturally drawn to, along with what seems to repel you. Honor both sides of the truth spectrum as you discover your personal and authentic preferences.

JOURNAL PROMPTS

- What was your first thought when you were asked to choose your food?

- Did you find this exercise triggering? What conflicting emotions did you experience?

- Did you enjoy your time spent eating? Why do you think that is?

- If possible, invite someone to dine with you and practice this activity together. Compare and contrast with each other and discuss the similarities or differences you both experience.

"SO LONG AS YOU HAVE
FOOD IN YOUR MOUTH
YOU HAVE SOLVED
ALL PROBLEMS FOR
THE TIME BEING."
—FRANZ KAFKA

Homeopathic

We've already discussed the damaging effects our thoughts have on the way we assimilate our food. But what if we could use those negative feelings to help bring about a shift toward positive? The theory behind homeopathy is that like cures like. What might normally make someone ill in a large dose can potentially help another in a small dose. And now we're going to harness the transformative power behind the "law of similarities" in our eating habits!

I want you to think about how food makes you feel. Remember though, fat isn't a feeling. What we're looking for is an emotional response. Maybe there's a specific meal that reminds you of your childhood, when there wasn't enough food to go around. Are you worried or afraid there will never be enough? Or perhaps you're angry, because you were never allowed to eat more when you were still hungry.

Another option is to identify a reoccurring thought pattern that you're continually faced with. This can be related to your food story, or it can also be something that repeatedly shows up for you in any life lesson. For example, it could be a belief that you're invisible and that no matter what you say or do (or eat), no one will recognize your hard work.

In either case, once you've discovered a strong emotion you're wanting to transform, write it down along with its antithesis.

When you eat, the first couple of bites you'll focus on the negative. You'll then fill the remainder of your food with the desired emotion. Let's say you want to shift from fear to faith, or from anger to joy. The next time you sit down for a snack, take a few nibbles of fear/anger, and then finish it up with faith/joy. Doing so allows you to validate the negative before moving on to the positive and embracing it as your new reality.

JOURNAL PROMPTS

- What was your first thought when you were asked to transform your food?

- Did you find this exercise triggering? What conflicting emotions did you experience?

- Did you enjoy your time spent eating? Why do you think that is?

- Did you notice the food changing in any way as you shifted from negative to positive? For example, it tasted bitter at first and then started tasting sweet...

- If possible, invite someone to dine with you and practice this activity together. Compare and contrast with each other and discuss the similarities or differences you both experience.

Just Breathe

One of the most panic-inducing questions is "what's for dinner?" It's hard to decide because there's so much to consider! It seems like there are two main groups people fall into with regards to food: those who know what they should be eating but can't or won't, and those who don't know how because they're so inundated, confused and conflicted with all the information out there. Instead of listening to outside sources tell you what to eat, pay attention to your inner gut wisdom. If you start to feel overwhelmed or unfocused, take a moment and assess your breath. Which nostril are you breathing out of? Switch your breath, switch your thoughts.

Right nostril breathing will give you more energy and focus. Left nostril breathing will help you calm down and relax. And then there's Nadi Shodhan, or alternate nostril breathing. Excellent for grounding, a daily routine of alternate nostril breathing done first thing in the morning and right before bedtime will keep you present, mindful, and centered. It does a fabulous job of helping you process both negative and positive emotions. Also great throughout the day whenever you're in need of a "time-out." And it just so happens to be one of my favorite ways to experience food!

Take a moment to rehearse alternate nostril breathing before adding in the food element. First, block your right nostril and inhale through the left. Now, block your left nostril and exhale through the right. Next, inhale through the right nostril before blocking it and exhaling out the left nostril. Repeat the process. Continue to alternate your inhalation and exhalation by switching nostrils as described.

For this particular activity, identify a specific food item that you love and another food that you hate. Practice alternate nostril breathing with your "love food" for three minutes. Journal whatever comes up for you. Then take another three minutes and breathe with your "hate food." Write down any thoughts or feelings you have and notice if a shift has taken place.

Generally speaking, the second round of alternate nostril breathing with the dreaded food is more difficult for most people. Rest assured that it does get better as the seconds tick by! It may seem like it lasts forever, but I promise that the timer will eventually go off at the end of three minutes. So close your eyes and just breathe. Allow your breath to help process the wave of emotions that rise and fall.

You may also realize that what you thought was a love food is actually a hate food, such as chocolate, due to the shame attached to it. Maybe you find your hate food more tolerable after breathing with it. If you notice that one nostril is more blocked than the other and makes switching nostrils difficult, then simply sit with your chosen foods while you connect with your breath. Perhaps you'd like to experiment with breathing through a single nostril, depending on how you're feeling about things. However you approach this exercise, and whatever the end result might be, trust that you are experiencing it for your highest good.

JOURNAL PROMPTS

- What was your first thought when you were asked to breathe your food?

- Did you find this exercise triggering? What conflicting emotions did you experience?

- Did you notice the food changing in any way as the minutes passed by? For example, it smelled potent at first and then started smelling pleasant...

- If possible, invite someone to dine with you and practice this activity together. Compare and contrast with each other and discuss the similarities or differences you both experience.

{ SPIRIT }

Say Grace

Many times people confuse spirituality with religion, and they're not the same thing. Quite often, and ideally speaking, one's chosen religion is a form of spiritual practice. But you don't have to be religious to be spiritual. You are Spirit, period. There's more to you than flesh and blood. And there's more to your food than calories and macronutrients.

For my part, I'm Christian and I have an intimate relationship with my Faith. You do NOT have to share my beliefs in order to benefit from this workbook or these exercises. Please, whenever I refer to a specific spiritual entity substitute your Higher Power — whether that's Mother Earth, the Universe, the Collective Consciousness or simply Source. All are welcome.

With that being said, it's important that we infuse our physical food with positive energy. For some, that might be blessing the food with the belief that the Atonement of Jesus Christ redeems our fallen food. You can still benefit from the metaphysical effects of prayer without subscribing to the Christian faith, for there is power in visualizing the breakfast or dinner table as complete and whole as we collectively express gratitude for the prepared meal.

For today, pause before each meal or snack and offer a blessing of gratitude. Give thanks for all that went into this meal's preparation. Trace it back, all the way to its origins and bless each part of its journey. While focusing on the positive before us, we can magnify the positive within us.

JOURNAL PROMPTS

- What was your first thought when you were asked to bless your food?

- Did you find this exercise triggering? What conflicting emotions did you experience?

- Did you enjoy your time spent eating? Why do you think that is?

- How did you feel about your meal as a whole?

- Were you able to recognize your part as a greater whole?

> *"The struggle ends when gratitude begins."*
> *—Neale Donald Walsch*

Potential

We can choose to see the negative or positive in life. "Don't judge a book by its cover," another popular saying, teaches us the importance of seeing with both our physical and spiritual eyes. Our sense of self, whether it's confidence or the lack thereof, is rooted in what we believe. In other words, our individual courage comes from truly seeing who we are and what role we play in the grand scheme of things.

Building off the values of connection and creation, courage continues the cycle of self-fulfillment. Being brave requires a firm grasp on both what is and what can be, while finding resolution in choosing the reality we desire most in the present moment. I can't help but think of the fairytale story of *Jack and the Beanstalk*. Here was a simple, poor farm boy who saw the great potential in a tiny bean. When that little bean turned into a giant gateway to a bigger world, he didn't cut it down or ignore it. He believed in himself and literally rose to the occasion. He made a better life for himself because he saw what he was and what he could be.

Just as important as seeing your food for what it is and where it came from is recognizing its potential to become something even more. A tiny mustard seed grows into a massive tree. Even rotten fruit has a purpose as a breeding ground for life.

When you are planning your meals and shopping for items on your grocery list, map out the life cycle of your food. Where does it come from, why is it here and where is it going? It doesn't just magically appear on your plate and disappear in the dishwasher (or toilet). What part does it play in your life, in the world at large, and how do you fit in? Identify how food can support you in your role, and how you can support it in its role.

JOURNAL PROMPTS

- What was your first thought when you were asked to map out your food?

- Did you find this exercise triggering? What conflicting emotions did you experience?

- Did you enjoy your time spent pondering/researching and why?

- Was it difficult to think about your food reflectively? If so, why?

- How did you feel about your meals before, during, and after wondering?

- Was it easier or harder to enjoy eating when you knew where it came from, or where it's going? Did you look forward to meal time?

> "You can soar if you find out
> who you are and why you are here."
> –Elaine Cannon

Harvest

I've said it before and I'll say it again: I love food! From the ground up. If you've never had the opportunity and pleasure to grow your own garden, then now is your chance. Get to know your food from seedling to entree. It is one of the best methods to feel connected with Self and Source.

Start with something small, like an herb garden, before graduating to a backyard crop. If you lack the space, enroll in a nearby community garden. If you lack the time, volunteer to help at your local Community Supported Agriculture (CSA).

One of the most fun ways to reconnect with food is doing it on its own terms. Mother Nature has provided us with a beautiful playground with room to grow and treasures to harvest. I'm not referring to groomed gardens, I'm referring to those often overlooked weeds and wild flora! Dandelions, plantain, and purslane. Salmon berries, huckleberries and salal. The tender white tips of carefully pulled grass blades. The sticky sap from trees that magically turns to chewing gum. Nectar from honey suckles. And the list goes on.

Have you ever asked yourself while standing in the produce section how that coconut got there or those beet greens came to be edible? I often wonder about the brave soul who discovered that tomatoes weren't poisonous after all, or that curious spirit who realized nuts were worth cracking. The next time you're walking through your yard or strolling in the park, look around and notice Nature's bounty. Grab a field guide and learn the joys of wildcrafting.

Recognize the potential each plant has as well as its innate divinity. Allow this truth to reflect back what lies dormant within you, letting your own inner divinity grow and flourish into what it's meant to be.

> "When one tugs at a single thing
> in nature, he finds it attached
> to the rest of the world."
> —John Muir

JOURNAL PROMPTS

- What was your first thought when you were asked to plant/harvest your food?

- Did you find this exercise triggering? What conflicting emotions did you experience?

- Did you enjoy your time spent cultivating and why?

- Was it difficult to think about your food naturally? If so, why?

- How did you feel about your food item before, during, and after planting/harvesting?

- Was it easier or harder to enjoy eating when you knew where it came from? Did you look forward to meal time?

"EVERYBODY NEEDS BEAUTY
AS WELL AS BREAD,
PLACES TO PLAY IN
AND PRAY IN, WHERE
NATURE MAY HEAL
AND GIVE STRENGTH
TO BODY AND SOUL."
–JOHN MUIR

Pen Pal

We have so many opportunities to communicate in this day and age such as via phone calls, emails, instant messaging and texting. Staying in touch with my old Pen-Pal from Germany would be so much easier nowadays… But when's the last time you sat down to write a letter by hand? I don't know a single person who doesn't still enjoy getting something in the mail! There's just something special about an intimate exchange between loved ones through pen and paper.

Maybe you still write your spouse or kids little love notes. Awesome. How often do you get a thank you card in return, from family or friends? Well, today it's your turn and it starts with you. There are a few different options, and there is no right or wrong way to do this assignment. You're welcome, as always, to modify this particular challenge to fulfill your personal needs. Be open to new discoveries and rekindled relationships.

You may choose to write a thank you card to yourself from your food, or you can draft a letter to your food from you. Even better, create a back and forth conversation between you and your food, almost like you used to do back in junior high with a best friend. Make the notes as lengthy or as short and sweet as you'd like. Feel free to ask questions, and then answer them.

It may seem a little bizarre at first, especially if you're playing both roles as sender and receiver. But you might surprise yourself and learn something new by reading what you've penned.

Journal Prompts

- What was your first thought when you were asked to write to your food?

- Did you find this exercise triggering? What conflicting emotions did you experience?

- Did you enjoy your time spent writing/reading and why?

- Was it difficult to think about your food responsively? If so, why?

- How did you feel about your food item before, during, and after writing?

> "We write to taste life twice,
> in the moment and in retrospect."
> —Anaïs Nin

Poetry Jam

Ah, poetry. I just love to read, analyze and embody poems. There are so many levels of understanding in written prose, and it's almost like a treasure hunt trying to decipher the clues and hidden meanings. It's particularly entertaining when one reader's take away completely varies from another's, especially if the author meant to take his readers in a totally different direction from the one they're currently heading.

Food is the same. It's far more complex than we give it credit for. Yes, antioxidants matter. So do minerals, amino acids, alkalinity, etc. But food isn't just a conglomerate of carbohydrates, proteins, and phytochemicals. It also acts as a vehicle for our thoughts and emotions. The way we experience our food is deeply symbolic and is full of explorative possibilities! What does food mean to YOU?

Express your feelings about food in poetry form. It can be as formulaic or abstract as you desire. If rhyming is your thing, go for it! Be silly and come up with some crazy puns or channel Dr. Seuss and make up ridiculous words. Maybe you're more comfortable following a haiku format. That's cool, too. Whatever moves your inner poet, find your inspiration and then let it flow. Before you know it, you'll have a sonnet.

Journal Prompts

- What was your first thought when you were asked to write about your food?

- Did you find this exercise triggering? What conflicting emotions did you experience?

- Did you enjoy your time spent composing and why?

- Was it difficult to think about your food lyrically? If so, why?

- How did you feel about your food item before, during, and after writing?

> "Poetry is the art of uniting
> pleasure with truth."
> —Samuel Johnson

Sing Along

Whether you're jamming out in your car to your favorite tunes on the radio or quietly sitting in your room and soaking up melodies that speak to your soul, music is a powerful force. Like food, it's another universal language. Even though some of us might not be fortunate enough to own or a play a musical instrument, almost everyone has a voice. We hum and rock our babies to sleep. We get together with friends for a memorable night of karaoke. We find ourselves glued to the screen in amazement as talented artists share a piece of their soul with us.

Before a meal or snack of your choice, sing a song. Croon away at your cereal. Serenade your salad. Pacify your pizza with a soothing lullaby. Pour your heart and soul into a love ballad meant just for your food. You can come up with your own tune, using your previously penned poetry as lyrics. Or choose a hymn, mantra or even a rousing rock song that best represents how you feel (or want to feel) about the food before you. Feel free to adlib and come up with something on the fly! Have fun and enjoy the moment with your food. Together, you can make some beautiful music.

Journal Prompts

- What was your first thought when you were asked to sing to/about your food?

- Did you find this exercise triggering? What conflicting emotions did you experience?

- Did you enjoy your time spent composing and why?

- Was it difficult to think about your food lyrically? If so, why?

- How did you feel about your food item before, during, and after singing?

> "Music is Life. That's why
> our hearts have beats."
> —Cecily Morgan

Perfect Plate

People make mistakes. We're perfectly imperfect. Good people can — and do — choose poorly. Sometimes we have this underlying fear that if we love someone, then we are condoning their behavior. When what we're truly afraid of is that we ourselves are unlovable for the mistakes we make.

Let me make this clear: your worth does not change.

The decisions you make may define you as a person, yet they do not define your worth as an individual. At our core, we are all the same. We are divine beings full of potential and worthy of love. Everyone is unique, and everyone has something to contribute. Yes, even you. Because you don't have to be perfect to have a message worth sharing.

Before you can change the world, transform the way you feel about yourself first. Time to raid your kitchen cabinets! Not for food, silly. For dining ware. Choose your fanciest bowl and use it as an offering for your next meal. You can use a special plate throughout the day, or save it for a specific snack. Go the extra mile and set the table using your nicest table cloth and finest china. Polish those antique silver spoons you inherited from your grandma and dig in. Practice plating your food as if you were a skilled chef at a famous restaurant. Try adding a sprig of parsley or sprinkle some coarse salt over your dish and enjoy.

Maybe you're used to saving all your niceties for company, but there's no need to wait because YOU are worth it now.

JOURNAL PROMPTS

- What was your first thought when you were asked to plate your food?

- Did you find this exercise triggering? What conflicting emotions did you experience?

- Did you enjoy your time spent presenting and why?

- Was it difficult to think about your food fancifully? If so, why?

- How did you feel about your food item before, during, and after plating?

> "Don't save something for a special occasion. Every day of your life is a special occasion."
> –Thomas S. Monson

I Am, I Am

What we focus on becomes our reality. If we focus on the negative, or all the ways we are different from each other, that is all we'll ever see. I choose to focus, and therefore see, what we all have in common. We're all here for connection. As human beings we're wired for connection. And we find that in being connected to our True Selves, our community, our family, and our Higher Power.

According to the Bible, "I Am" is one of the many names of Christ. Whenever we use the words "I am" in a negative way, we are essentially using the Lord's name in vain. I am statements are powerful, and the words we choose can either praise God or denounce Him. We are His children! What you say, or think, about yourself is meaningful and reflective of how you see your divinity.

So, who are you? This is best done by hand, so grab a pen or pencil and a sheet of paper. Set the timer for 1-3 minutes and write down everything that comes to mind, creating two columns: one for negative statements and one for positive. From these beliefs create a list of "I am" statements, but change the negative statements into positive statements. For example, if you wrote in your negative column something to the effect of "I am lazy" you will switch out that negative thought pattern for a positive one, such as "I am peace." Keep these statements short and sweet, ideally to a single value. I've provided a list of values for you to refer to, in case you struggle with finding the right words.

Now, for part two of your assignment. With your positive values in one hand, sit down with a snack in the other. Before each bite, read one of your new thought patterns and envision the food embodying, representing and symbolizing the positive value. Let's say you're eating a banana, or a cookie even. As you bring it to your mouth, close your eyes and imagine yourself literally eating peace. Continue to eat your food with an attached value to each bite. When you have finished your meal, sit still for a moment and feel yourself full of light.

JOURNAL PROMPTS

- What was your first thought when you were asked to complete this task?

- Did you find this exercise triggering? Any conflicting emotions?

- Did you enjoy your time spent eating? Why do you think that is?

- How did it feel eating values? Were you more satiated than normal?

> "You've been criticizing yourself for years and it hasn't worked. Try approving of yourself and see what happens."
> -Louise Hay

Focus Fast

There are several different ways to fast: going without food or water, or mono fasts such as a veggie fast, fruit fast and water fast. There are also several reasons to fast, especially to detox. Detoxing is almost as popular a phrase as clean eating. Cleanses are also known as a way to eliminate toxins, physically and spiritually. For many fasting is a spiritual practice. Unfortunately, there are those who approach cleanses with wild abandon.

Whenever someone tells me they're experimenting with a detox, my spider senses tingle and I immediately go on the defense with a single question: why? If you find yourself drawn to the latest detox fad, ask yourself why. If it's to lose weight, then stop right there. Perhaps you feel like a fast would help support a healthier liver or colon. In either case, before you start limiting food, get clear on your why.

Every time we remove something from our lives, we need to be mindful of what we're replacing the now empty space with. Instead of focusing on the foods that are forbidden, focus on the foods that are encouraged. And above all else, be present with not only your physical sensations but also your mental, spiritual and emotional. We are too quick to remove ourselves from food without removing ourselves from toxic environments, relationships or internal beliefs about ourselves.

I also want to point out the importance of taking care of yourself during the pre-cleanse phase as well as the post-cleanse phase. For example, don't start or end your fast with a steak dinner and leftover Halloween candy! It will confuse your body and possibly trap all those toxins you've worked so hard to release. Please, get a support system or sponsor for any cleanse and definitely ease yourself into and out of it gently.

Think of it like giving birth: you have Braxton Hicks and contractions (pre-cleanse) that build up to the labor/delivery and final push (cleanse), and then you rest for 6-8 weeks while your body heals and you adjust to your new normal (post-cleanse). You would NEVER go and run a marathon the day after giving birth! So please be careful, listen to your body and get help. You might also want to consider mini-cleanses or the occasional weekend tune-up afterward to maintain the positive benefits of a major seasonal cleanse.

For this particular exercise I'm not necessarily suggesting you go on a typical fast. You decide on what you want to focus on today. It could range from something as simple as consuming nothing but green drinks and salads. Or perhaps you'd like to try something completely radical and illogical such as an atypical sugar fast — where you actually eat sweets all day, as opposed to avoiding them. You decide. What do you need less of? And more importantly, what do you need more of? Get centered, and find your focus.

JOURNAL PROMPTS

- What was your first thought when you were asked to fast?

- Did you find this exercise triggering? What conflicting emotions did you experience?

- Did you enjoy your time spent eating, or not eating? Why do you think that is?

- How did you feel about your food after completing this assignment?

- By focusing on one aspect, were you able to experience yourself as a whole?

> "In this modern age, I think we can take "detox" into a renewed meaning of carving out the quiet space within our busy everyday lives to get clear on what nourishes, replenishes, and supports our whole self."
> –Deanna Minich

Meditate

According to Pam Blackwell, "the term meditation refers to a broad variety of practices that includes techniques designed to promote relaxation, build internal energy or life force [...] and develop compassion, love, patience, generosity and forgiveness." As I've mentioned before, Kundalini Yoga & Meditation has played a pivotal role in how I see myself and others. I have found it extremely effective at working on all levels of health, and as I've kept up with my practice it has kept me going through thick and thin. There are several mindfulness modalities, and I encourage you to find a practice that resonates with you most and then bring it to the table.

For now, I invite you to experiment with a simple fruit meditation:

1. Pick something that you can easily hold in your hand for a few minutes. An apple, orange or banana would be great whereas a watermelon might be too heavy!

2. Grab a pen and notepad.

3. Find a quiet place free from distractions.

4. Sit comfortably in a chair with your feet on the ground. You may also choose to channel your inner

yogi and sit lotus style on the floor (use a pillow or blanket to help elevate your hips). Sit nice and tall with a straight spine, your chin gently tucked.

5. Hold your fruit in your left hand. Depending on how it's grown and where its point of origin is will determine what direction to face the fruit. For example, if you were to use an apple, its stem is its connection to its source (tree). Rest the apple on its side in your palm, facing the stem outward.

6. Close your eyes and imagine that you are completing the circuit between the fruit and its source. Ask the fruit to tell you a little about itself. Without judgment, write down any words, thoughts, or feelings that come to mind.

7. When you are done, take a deep breath and thank your food for teaching you. Give it a kiss, fill it with gratitude and love. You may choose to eat it, gift it to a friend, or return it to its resting place until you're ready to enjoy it.

Feel free to repeat this exercise with multiple fruits, and see how differently they respond to you. You may also try this with vegetables, or any other food item you feel called to communicate with. For an extra challenge, practice meditating with something you identify as a "bad food" — because, it's important to recognize that we all come from the same Source. Remember, everyone and everything is part of a Greater Whole. If you find this surprisingly difficult, that's ok! As I tell all my yoga students, please do your best and honor where you're at today. There is no competition here, just you tuning in to your personal sacred space. Go at your own pace and simply enjoy uniting your food with your body, mind, emotions and spirit.

JOURNAL PROMPTS

- What was your first thought when you were asked to meditate with your food?

- Did you find this exercise triggering? What conflicting emotions did you experience?

- Did you enjoy your time spent receiving and recording?

- Was it difficult to think about your food responsively? If so, why?

- How did you feel about your food item before, during, and after meditating?

> "We are not human beings
> having a spiritual experience,
> we are spiritual beings
> having a human experience."
> −Pierre Teilhard de Chardin

Feast Journey II

Now we've come full circle! Forty or so days ago you started this exploratory food journey with a guided imagery journey. This time I want you to listen to it again and evaluate what has changed for you.

True Food: Feast Journey –
Banquet Hall Guided Meditation

https://www.youtube.com/watch?v=cdh3eNH spQc&feature=youtu.be

- Have you noticed a shift in your perception of food?

- Do you find that your fears and struggles have been replaced with hope or peace?

- Has your relationship with yourself morphed into something brighter?

"MAY THE LONG TIME SUN
SHINE UPON YOU,
ALL LOVE SURROUND YOU,
AND THE PURE LIGHT WITHIN YOU
GUIDE YOUR WAY ON."
—FAREWELL BLESSING

{ Epilogue }

I spent three days in Utah, with about fifty other women, learning and growing beyond anything I believed possible. That's what happens at a Quickening event. Luckily for me, my role was one of meal prepper and food facilitator — something I loved and felt comfortable doing. Having planned the meals and experiences in advance, I thought I knew what to expect. But I was wrong.

Before arriving at my destination, a dear friend gave me some words of encouragement as well as a voice of caution. She intuited that I would have to stand up for truth. As I dutifully played my part that weekend, I nervously kept my eyes and ears open for an opportunity to present itself. Not because I wanted to create conflict, but so that I could be prepared to diffuse any if necessary. I'm often known as the designated peacemaker and was therefore ready to step forward as needed.

The food was admittedly delicious and everyone seemed to enjoy themselves. In fact, several participants expressed their appreciation and raved about how healthy they thought everything was. More than once, I heard comments about the foods' ability to raise their vibration. All of this was great news, for it was exactly what I planned! I wanted the food to be supportive of their highest good. My intention was to help people heal from the inside out, and food has always been my tool of choice. However, I began to feel unsettled. And then I had an impression that shook me to my core.

While I was cleaning up dinner, I started to mentally prepare for breakfast the next day — our last meal together. The original plan was to provide an oatmeal bar, with fun and nutritious toppings. I had noticed that a lot of the women were self-conscious about eating sugar or processed foods, and I was worried that a topping such as chocolate chips or whipped cream wouldn't be acceptable. I had also realized that the dressings, sauces, and other ingredients from previous meals were less than ideal and I began to panic about what others would think... It was then that I had a random, outrageous, and truly terrifying idea suddenly occur to me: what if instead of oatmeal, I offered cold cereal? Not the healthy kind, but the processed junk full of sugar, food dye, and ingredients unpronounceable.

My panic went into overdrive! It was ridiculous. I could not, in good faith, recommend someone eat something like that. I'm a nutritionist, for crying out loud! I almost brushed it off completely until a quiet inner voice reminded me of my friend's previous warning and then proceeded to teach me that there is no good food or bad food, just food. The way we judge food is synonymous with the way we judge ourselves. Everything, and everyone, has value.

This was what I needed to learn. This was what I was expected to share. Cold cereal would act as a trigger point, an opportunity to teach the truth — that even though we might be flawed or incomplete, we are still enough. We are still worth loving.

The following morning I woke up literally sick to my stomach. I had my doubts, and I was insanely nervous. But I knew I had to follow through with the prompting. So I did. After teaching yoga and meditation, I began to set up the breakfast table. Eyes widened as women recognized what was happening, their alarm and disbelief almost matching my own. Finally, all was ready.

With a deep breath, I stood in front of these women and told the truth. That not all of the ingredients over the past couple of days were nutrient dense. As a visitor from out of town, and having traveled by plane, I was therefore unable to make everything from scratch. Out of necessity, I had settled for chicken bouillon, bottled dressings, packaged salads, etc. And while I would have loved to provide them with the best foods possible, the truth was simple: I loved them, I loved the food I was preparing, and that love was what they were consuming.

The rest of my message from that fateful day can be found in the preface of this workbook. On the plane ride home, I received a divine download as explained in the "Getting Started: Why 40 Days" section. At the time, it was all new to me. But a fire had been lit and the flames were fanned as I realized our sensitive ties with food.

After that, I finally embraced my calling as a food guru who creates meal plans, wellness programs and food experiences with one goal in mind: to help explore, and ultimately heal, our relationship with food and self. Looking back, there isn't anything I would change about my journey. And now I want to help others with their journeys.

When I committed to writing this book, my paradigm continued to shift. I discovered something called "the psychology of eating" and it blew me away! I realized there must be a key component we've been missing all along, and I believe it has less to do with what we eat and more to do with HOW we relate to our food.

I'm so grateful for the things I've learned and for the opportunity I have to share these truths to anyone willing to listen.

There is power in slowing down, in being present in our body while we enjoy and savor our food. What a gift we've been given, this need for food! When we take the time to listen to our body's cues we find ourself eating several times a day. Our lives are so hectic, especially nowadays. How fascinating it is that we have this built-in reminder to slow down. Which means we have the opportunity to nourish our whole self, to pause and reflect, to receive the answers we've been looking for, to remember who we are and realize our true potential.

Food is a gift. We need it. Your life is a gift. We need you, too.

{ Personal Stories }

In asking for willing guinea pigs to experiment with this workbook, I was able to gather some evidence as to how powerful experiential eating is. It was interesting how many people would later back out, due to time constraints or essentially discomfort over what I was asking them to do. And I don't blame them! I do this to myself all the time. My relationship with food is often placed on the back burner, too. Like most people, I also fall prey to the have-to-do's: I *have* to answer this text/email, check my newsfeed, watch this show, fold the laundry, run errands, etc. The truth is I *have* to eat. If we don't eat, we die. It's as plain and simple as that.

So I ask myself, and I invite you to do the same: How am I choosing to spend my time?

Even if it doesn't feel like it, there is always a choice. For me, when I choose to be present with my food and bodies — physical, mental, emotional and spiritual — I'm more complete, more whole. I'm more Me. If I truly *have* to eat, I might as well make it meaningful! Instead of suffering through a necessary life requirement, I want to enjoy it. What do you want?

Eating is a great way to introduce myself to myself. As I've studied about the importance of choice and desire, I've realized that it applies to not only areas in our life such as sex or entertainment, but also to our food. The next time you eat, ask yourself: "What do I desire?" It can be something simple like, "I desire hot chocolate, because I'm cold" or it can be something deeper, such as "I desire hot chocolate, because it reminds me of my grandparent's cabin. I'm lonely, and I miss them." When you identify your heart's desire, validate it. Then make a choice.

Quite often our feelings and emotions just need to be heard. Instead of eating to numb out, tune in to what you want. You're hungry for something; listen up and find your why.

Jamie

This challenge came at a great time. The relationship with food for me is a struggle. My family had always showed affection through food. In fact, so much so every family gathering and reunion we are all stuffed to the brim and then some. My husband's family eats to survive. Feelings are often hurt of those who joined the family because we put in a lot of time and effort and love to make great dishes and desserts and they often go untouched.

Anyhow, I have been dealing personally with body/diet issues and am trying to find a happy medium between being healthy, but enjoying life and letting food focus and exercise take over every second of my day. I also just watched the Embrace documentary that goes along with this thinking. I loved a lot of what they were saying.

All of that being said, I tried to use other senses as I ate. I usually categorize my plate or meal in order from what I like least to most. I didn't realize I did that. The problem I found was that in recipes where there are ingredients I didn't care for I would pick things out and either eat them real quick or discard them. But that changes the flavor of things. In trail mix I would pick out the raisins and save the M&M's for last, etc. So when I got this challenge the first thing I tried was yogurt and cottage cheese. A friend of mine told me this is how she gets extra protein. So being that I'm not a huge fan of cottage cheese I closed my eyes and ate up. I enjoyed it. It smelled good and I actually liked the texture, but by closing my eyes I didn't know what I was getting. It was a pleasant surprise.

I love the smell of sautéed onions, but am not an onion fan so this trick works well in any dish that includes them. The smell is glorious and the taste is great as long as there isn't a crunch to go with. Anyhow I've been trying to savor my food and appreciate it more for all of the different tastes as well as getting the nutrients that my body needs, and wants!

Janessa

The biggest thing I noticed was how hard it actually was to take the time to slow down and actually taste/smell my food. I feel like I'm so busy that eating has just become something on a check list and not something I was enjoying every time I ate. I'm trying to change that now and actually enjoy the different smells and tastes in every food. I had never done that before.

It was a wakeup call for me to slow down and simplify my life so I could actually enjoy the things I get to do daily.

Jennifer

I love smelling my food. I cook and buy by smell so this is easy for me. I was triggered in a good way, with fond memories and connections to the past. I felt mostly gratitude for the food and everything about it — feelings of wishing the food was in its natural state and not modified by man or processed. I feel like I'm losing my sense of taste... I can smell all the wonderful flavors as I cook but don't taste them like I want to when I eat.

Being alone with 5 kids, we all still sit down and eat for breakfast, lunch and dinner. Most of the time I enjoy it — though I am rushed more than I would like to be. Time and place and season for everything. I think I enjoy time I spend eating because it is together time. A time to nourish body and relationships with family and with tradition and with God. I enjoy the one daily task that really makes me feel good completing (most of the time).

I do appreciate processed food and their smells. And I get great joy from eating said food, too. But smelling food — all kinds, even organic — turns my thoughts to wishing for food to be more as God intended... perhaps the real challenge would be to smell it and see the food I am eating to BE the food God intended for me. I desire the food right out of Eden, so full of life.

I wish to have my food right out of my back yard... seeing as how I grow nothing but grass and a few edible sprouts right now means I must content myself with food from other sources. So if I was to dig deep, I would say that the bigger challenge for me would be to show true gratitude for my food as it is instead of praying over it and asking God to remove the pesticides and the chemicals and asking God to give me the highest benefit it can... to just instead say, "Thank You."

We eat frozen pizza once in a while, refined sugar once in a while, meat and other things once in a while, and we enjoy them and appreciate having them... but even with my fresh organic stuff I wish in a small way that it came from God's garden. In some ways it feels like I'm grateful for all food 99% but hold that last bit of regret that whatever I'm eating be it apple or cake that it isn't perfect or as I imagine God intended it to be... I am not sure why I do this other than I do have a desire to eat Godly food. I'm glad I don't have this issue with other creations of God.

Nathan

My initial thought was that this could be interesting, but I wasn't expecting it to increase (or decrease) my experience. I did find I enjoyed my food while listening, especially when crunching away on fresh fruits and vegetables. They seem more fresh and healthy when I am hearing that crunch. It is very satisfying.

The sounds of food, both in its preparation and consumption, definitely contribute to one's experience, toward the better or worse. Foods can indeed sound fresh and healthy, whether it be the crunch of a carrot or the pop you get from biting into a grape tomato.

Diana

I have to admit that I didn't actually write out a list. I know, I know. I'm like that person on a recipe site who says, "Great recipe — I substituted applesauce for oil, and added flour instead of sugar" which all could change the results dramatically. That being said, I did think about some fundamental negative statements I seem to hold and focused on the inverse of those.

My first thought when I was asked to complete this task was kind of mixed emotions. First, I have faith in your way of thinking here, and felt this could really turn out to be a positive thing if I took it seriously. Second, I questioned faith in my ability to actually take it seriously.

I WAYYYYYY enjoyed my time spent eating far better when consciously focusing on the positive statements. I felt there was a natural inclination to slow down and focus on what I was eating as a result of the exercise. I know I am a fast eater and this significantly slowed me down. I actually got to enjoy what I was eating instead of just scarfing it down and enjoying the after taste. Also, by slowing down, it wasn't like I was missing out by eating slower. The food didn't get cold. There was still food left when I was ready for more, etc. (all contributing factors as to why I think I eat fast. I grew up competing against 8 people at the dinner table for what I wanted).

I don't know if "eating values" was cause for satiation, or if my awareness of being satiated was more obvious. I was even able to do this exercise when I was eating at the dinner table with other people. I thought of the value statement I wanted to reinforce before each bite and repeated it as I chewed. I felt corny at first, but I believe in the power of affirmative speaking so I got over the discomfort of doing something out of the box.

Elyssa

So I immediately resisted this idea. I actually snap pictures of my meals not infrequently because I think food is gorgeous, but for some reason I was initially bummed about my assignment. I guess I thought it was too easy and normal, ha! But once I started taking pictures of the entire process, I was instantly excited. There was an automatic shift in how I was thinking about my food — I was about 8 weeks postpartum and had had a rather difficult recovery with this baby; so I was just starting to get into cooking again for real, but I hadn't been jazzed about it. The first picture I took of the butt of our breakfast sourdough loaf my husband had baked the night before almost made me giddy; our food is so so beautiful! It's like I fell in love with it once I actually looked at it. And taking pictures of every step involved in feeding myself and my family helped me be in love with every ingredient. A bowl of sorted dried chickpeas literally took my breath away for a second.

I was also oddly more patient with letting my kids help prepare meals and thought it was fun to be able to document their work, from the garden to the cutting board to the stove top. I just felt more relaxed about everything, because food was the task of the day instead of something to get over with before our "real" tasks. So I was a much more fun and involved mom than my kids had had in a while.

Not only did I really enjoy the picture taking once I started, but I also noticed how much it changed how I ate that day. For one thing, knowing I'd have to take a picture of whatever I ate motivated me to eat things that would be pretty, and I realized that healthy, nourishing food is way more attractive than easy-access junk. I still grabbed some not-healthy snacks throughout the day, and I felt fine about it, but it was very easy to notice that those foods weren't nearly as pretty, and I felt their appeal decrease even before taking the picture. After several weeks of very mindless eating that led to many cravings for foods that didn't nourish, this was an interesting result.

All in all, I really enjoyed the assignment and even unofficially extended it a few days, taking pictures of particularly striking moments in my food prep that I otherwise might not have noticed. What was most surprising, however, was how it affected my relationship with my kids for the day as I allowed us to slow down and appreciate the beauty of our food and how lucky we are to be able to have the time and resources to enjoy such wonderful variety. It reminded me how healing food can be if we allow it. I was surprised by how grateful I felt, and that was definitely a welcome shift.

Going through the photos now, ironically I can see that I also spontaneously completed several things I'd been avoiding and actually had a much more productive day than I'd had in a while. I guess adding so much intention to one aspect of my day led to a much more energetic attentiveness to several others, as well!

Rebecca

My first thought when I was asked to save or leave some food was, "Oh, that is a great idea! But that will be hard!" I was raised to clean my plate, and with a big family there was sometimes competition for food and if you didn't ask for seconds quickly enough, there might not be any if you were still hungry. So it's hard to leave food on my plate. I mostly chose to do this exercise by saving some food to make a "perfect last bite." I thought it was a brilliant idea! I tend to create perfect bites of many meals, with a perfect combination of foods on each forkful. Every bite of pizza needs a piece of pineapple, and every bite of beans and rice needs a little lettuce and guac with it, haha. I often create a perfect first bite — I sit down and carefully choose exactly what looks yummy together. So why not a perfect last bite, too?

Sometime mid-meal, I would look at the food on my plate and think, hmm, what would be the perfect last bite? And then I'd save a little bit of each thing I wanted. When I ate pizza, I would cut off a chunk from the center of the slice so that my last bite wouldn't just be crust! Then when I was done, I'd have that last perfect bite to look forward to and really savor. It helped me eat more mindfully and enjoy the meal. It also helped me feel more satiated. I have a sweet tooth and often right after I eat, I have a huge sugar craving and want something sweet to top it off. But by saving myself a Perfect Bite to finish my meal with instead, I found that I didn't need sugar or anything else. I felt more satisfied. I did this many times over the last few weeks and each meal when I did this felt more fulfilling — it helped me actually focus on the food, the taste, and use more of my senses and brain to eat mindfully. It was *more of a pleasant, holistic (mind and body) experience than just a habit of filling my tummy.*

It wasn't difficult to save food on my plate for a perfect last bite; it was actually fun to look forward to the perfect ending to my meal. And actually, as I've done this more often, I've occasionally found myself not cleaning my plate, but eating that perfect bite and being done before all the food is gone. It's not usually a large amount of food left uneaten (this morning it was just a couple bites of hot cereal, when I ran out of raisins and decided I didn't actually want to finish it all), but it's becoming easier to not have to clean my plate and give myself permission to do so without guilt.

I really enjoyed this exercise and have found myself eating more mindfully and enjoying the meals more. I have felt more satisfied and either not had seconds or had smaller seconds because I was paying more attention to my food and getting more pleasure from it.

Lacy

At first I thought it would be boring to just watch someone cook. I'm a talker, too, so knew it would be a challenge to keep my mouth shut. I chose to observe because I do most of the cooking, and wanted to experience seeing someone else take that care. I looked forward to it. It was hard to plan, and I felt myself avoid making it happen. To combat that, I just jumped in when my son was cooking, and observed form a distance.

I watched my oldest grill some hamburgers for the family. He's not a man of many words, so just kind of did his own thing anyway. He was meticulous in how he paid attention to the juices, dripping them onto the other hamburgers so they were not wasted. I was impressed at the care he took to make them perfect. I wanted to share the experience with him, but didn't want him to feel uncomfortable. It was hard for me to not be able to share that with him, and made me realize the distance I feel in our relationship. That distance is amplified when we are at the dinner table, so I felt sadness at watching him. I also felt great love, even awe at the man he is becoming. I really liked just seeing him do something he loved. He was so relaxed, and just a bigger, stronger version of the sweet little boy I once sang to sleep and comforted when he hurt. I miss that. This exercise helped me see the loneliness and hurt he feels after deep personal losses. I hurt for him, and just wanted to scoop him up and make it better. Instead, I let him prepare food for the family, and waited.

Things didn't go according to plan, and we didn't end up getting to eat together. I did really enjoy the meal, feeling the care he feels, but hides behind his insecurities and anger. It was easy to not speak, as he doesn't respond well to me most of the time. What ached was the distance I felt from him, and at the same time the deep desire to bridge that. It changed how I see him, and it changed how I see us. I have spent years trying to nourish and nurture him with what I cooked and baked. He loves to cook, and takes great joy in sharing his creations. My approval and enjoyment bring a rare smile to his face. In life we get so distracted. This didn't change anything for him, but for me I now see how much more than a physical need food is to a family. Tomorrow I will tell him how much that hamburger meant to me. It was the best one I've ever had.

Melisa

I realized that I need less green smoothies and more whole green foods. I noticed that I didn't feel the same feeling of "conquered" or maybe adrenaline as I do with green smoothies. I think this is because of media and culture approval. Eating whole green dishes is not as highly touted as green smoothies. Cooking veggies is not as highly praised as eating them raw. So even though my body was being thoroughly nourished, I wasn't feeling the "praise of the world" for doing it. It showed me that the voice of orthorexia does still exist and hold a little more weight than I would like it to, in my mind.

My first thought when I was asked to fast was, "I'm pregnant! I can't fast! I just need to focus on eating lots of everything!" Fasting is a little bit dangerous territory because I used to fast all the time without really planning on it, just starving all the time for control and coping.

I felt excited to eat more whole green foods but fear of eating enough because green smoothies make high quantity consumption easier because I don't have to think about eating or take as much time to prepare. I did enjoy my time spent eating. It felt nourishing to take that time for myself and I felt more connected to the food also, by taking time to prepare it in a nourishing way at a time during the day when I normally wouldn't prepare veggies.

I was treating the food like a gift and treating my body like a gift and treating the time spent preparing and eating the food as a self-care time instead of just rushing through my day with a big cup of greens in my hand that I hardly take the time to taste, let alone enjoy or appreciate. Also, I was surprised to discover that I had several yummy dishes to prepare that I really did enjoy. I usually assume that I don't really enjoy veggies, but I do, when they are prepared in a way that I like them. When I was eating the greens, I felt more connected with the present moment.

Kristen

It makes me anxious to think of food as fun. Eating is always so serious for me. It was difficult to let myself go. I thought about the project for weeks before I actually did it. After I started, I felt free.

I chose to eat the food I was playing with. At first, I didn't want to eat it because it didn't look like it "should." However, I ate it and it tasted just fine.

I did enjoy my time spent eating. Probably because I spent more time with my food than normal. Usually my plate is clear before I realize how much I've eaten. It was a good exercise for me.

Heather

This was a very difficult task for me. As long as I can remember, my mother would have to remind me to slow down and chew, and to this day I still will down food and be the first one to always finish a meal — so when you sent me this task I laughed!

It was very hard to remind myself. I had to put Post-it notes in my kitchen to remind me to slow down, chew and enjoy my food.

When I did it, it was amazing. I enjoyed my food more, it made me more relaxed, and I felt full sooner. Taking the time to pause a few seconds before I started eating made me really focus on the event of the meal and focus on the food.

I was more in tune with my body and what it was saying. I found that when I ate fast I wasn't listening to my body at all. I did enjoy eating much more and focused on the tastes more which made me enjoy the food more.

It was very difficult to slow down but once I did it was a whole different experience for me. It made me realize that my body is saying so much to me about my food and whether or not it needs more or not, and by going fast and mindlessly eating I was totally ignoring it.

I'm going to continue to try and do this as I believe it is so healthy to our body but our mind.

Leah

While doing my task, I didn't notice myself enjoying eating more neither did I find myself feeling more satiated than normal. It was also not triggering for me, but then again my relationship with food is pretty decent. However, in general, I have noticed that when I use positive thoughts I am a much happier and calmer person. When I focus on the positive, it forces my brain to be in the present so it doesn't spiral down a dark rabbit hole and focus on things that are triggering to me.

I decided to do the actual rice experiment to see what would happen. Both my "love" rice and my "hate" rice ended up getting some mold on it after a week, though the "hate" rice had its mold spread out all over whereas the "love" rice had a few isolated spots. While conducting the experiment, I found I had a hard time hating the hate rice. I realized that that isn't me, my soul doesn't like to hate or say mean things.

But what really struck me is the fact that while I had a hard time being mean to rice, I don't have a hard time beating myself up in my head and using negative self-talk on a regular basis!?! That does not seem right! That was a huge eye opener for me. Sometimes we need to learn to treat ourselves more kindly, the way we treat other people. When you fully read and understand God's great commandments as found in Matthew 22:39 — "Thou shalt love thy neighbour as thyself" — you realize that part of the commandment is to love yourself. Negative self-talk is not helpful in the least bit.

Luana

As I contemplated writing a poem about food, I knew it would be something that would take some time. I love to write, so part of me was anxious and excited about the assignment, but the other part of me, the part that wants to always present the best I can be, was scared to undertake this assignment.

I've know that I have issues with food for quite some time, so I put off writing. I have several conflicting emotions. I want to be like everyone else and I don't want to be like everyone else are the conflicting thoughts I have in my mind. I watch people eat and eat ice cream, breads, cookies, and other things and they don't seem to suffer, but I suffer when I eat this way and I can't justify it, so I suffer in other ways.

Thoughts of food are always triggering me. I'm triggered to guilt, shame, and disgust, I am also triggered to thoughts like: Will this make me sick? Will I regret this? Surely I can allow myself some room to enjoy what I like?

As I began to write my poem, I allowed myself to do an honest portrayal of the thoughts that plague me. I think I condensed it into just the negative aspects for me, but I do find joy in good food. I just didn't know how to write that also without nullifying what truly goes on for me emotionally. That's more why I hesitated to write. I try hard to not just present the negative in my life, because I am also a joyful, happy person. And.... Here I am trying to justify and not have me look a particular way to anyone. Knowing this about myself, makes me want to cry.

I stood in the grocery store today and made some decisions. I also worry about judgment from other people in my life who I'm responsible to feed and nourish with my meals. Yesterday Stella, (granddaughter age 3) was watching me fry some eggs for breakfast. She loves eggs and wanted one also. She sat by me on the counter and so sweetly asked, "Do you also have bacon?" Well, of course not, that's not good for us, was my thought. We haven't eaten pork for years and turkey bacon has sodium nitrate in it. I love turkey bacon and I feel fine when I eat it, but I don't get it very often. Maybe once a year. What's a person to do? I bought turkey bacon.

Joi

This is an amazing experience. I love to sing. I sing to the radio. I make up silly songs for my kids. Music brings the soul joy. Singing to my salad or about my salad wasn't that big of a stretch for this singing, Dr. Suess-ish person. I loved the idea right from the start.

I could see times when I wouldn't feel as comfortable singing about dinner. Some people make me more self-conscious. Their very presence would cause me to pull inside and lose that free spirit that sings to supper.

I loved it. Especially when my little ones are around. They get a kick out of the ridiculous things I might say — or the rhymes that don't come out quite right.

I struggle with food at times so for me this opportunity gave me a chance to change my relationship with food though music.

I was surprised at the change. I welcomed the experience openly, without shame. I sang to my heart and my mind. I sang for my body to welcome the food and to accept it and use it to nourish my body. I sang that I would find the meal tasty and that I would be able to want to eat what I prepared. I loved the peace singing presented to my body and to my meal.

Wonderful experience!

Lizzy

I have been thinking about this task all month and it has been wonderful as I think about the things I could say to my food for what it does for me (physically and emotionally). Thank you for letting me be a part of this, and I really enjoyed this exercise. I actually sat down and wrote tonight and it was really intriguing where this conversation went, so thank you for that opportunity.

I thought it would be different but once I could past the initial odd feelings, I knew I would like it. I love writing and I love how things just open up as you write.

I know I have emotional connections to food, but I also use it as a way to relate to other people. It is a comfort zone to me and I didn't realize how much I use food to connect and relate to other people. I discovered that part of that reason is it because it is something that everyone has in common. It is a basic need that every human who has and who will be needs and so we are connected by food.

I did enjoy my time spent writing. I have been thinking about it for a while but in writing I was able to really create the dialogue and it was very powerful.

At first, it was difficult to think about my food responsively, but once I could get over myself, it was really amazing. The counter dialogue was very spiritual as food was created to nourish our bodies. God created food and it is vital to our bodies, that were also created by God, so that we can have the *nourishment and strength to live and to fulfill Heavenly Father's purpose for us. I never would have connected the blessing of food in that way if I hadn't created the food response.*

My gratitude changed throughout the exercise. I was also able to identify ways that I connect with food that I hadn't realized. I also really thought more about what foods I choose and why and what my emotion is around some of those foods.

Allie

I've always loved the idea of gardening, but implementation has never been my strong suit! I plant a garden every year and am impressed with myself if I get a dozen edibles out of the whole thing.

This time around, I realized some of my issues around gardening for food. First, I realized that while I'm excited about gardening as a concept, I always find reasons not to give it 100%. I let myself skip days of watering, or I won't weed for way too long, and I feel guilty about that but then congratulate myself for having a garden at all. Then I also realized as my latest garden grew, that I felt guilty about eating what little each plant did produce, because it felt like I was killing the plant, and like I'd put in so much work for a few measly green beans, maybe I had better let them at least get a little teensy bit bigger before I picked them... I always found reasons to 1) not garden 100% and 2) not enjoy the fruits of my own garden, out of guilt.

This past time I grew my garden, I felt guilty about harvesting my one decent-sized vegetable. It felt like such a waste to finally harvest it and ruin the whole plant's life.

But then there was a hailstorm and I was having guests over for dinner.

I was making a salad and knew I needed that one single vegetable. I couldn't go to the store. The plant was going to die in the hail anyway. I ran out in my garden in the snow and ice and harvested the veggie, and then ran back in to wash it and chop it and finish making the salad.

It was good.

And I realized: I had nothing to feel guilty about. This plant's entire purpose was to create this single vegetable, for me. For my dinner party. For this salad. And it was happy to do it.

I shouldn't feel guilty for picking the fruits of my garden... I should feel guilty for NOT picking the fruits! This is how food fulfills its destiny. It is a servant and it loves its job.

It was a transformational moment for me.

I planted my spring garden this year, and honestly it all already died without producing. But I'll try again later this summer. And I won't feel guilty about my gardening failures, because at least I am trying, and I won't feel guilty about eating what I grow, because I know it's growing for me.

Becky

You asked me to make my shopping list then shake things up. So, I got up early on a week day and after taking my son to school and before going to work, I went to the store. I thought about what you said about buying something I would not normally buy and something fun or special. So, I bought organic hot dogs which I don't usually do because organic is usually so expensive and how do I know it's really organic? Then I threw in a bag of my favorite chips, sea salt and vinegar.

At the checkout I finally asked the woman I have seen many times why she wears a man's class ring on her necklace. Her son died shortly after high school and she wears it in his honor. I now love her even more! That made me so happy because she seemed to really be excited about sharing her story with me.

And…I realized…I really like going early in the morning. I feel happier, not run down (although I am usually still smiling when I shop even at the end of a long day). I have to tell you, the chips were hard to avoid once they were open and I really did not need them but they were so yummy. Oh, and the organic hot dogs were actually really good. Who knew?!

Ella

My assignment was to dress up my food pretty, break out the good dishes, plate things nicely, etc. When I first got my assignment I thought this would be so fun and easy. It was so easy that I kept putting it off, that was my first stumbling block. My next stumbling block was that I didn't trust my kids with the good dishes. Little kids and grandma's china just aren't a good mix. So then I thought I'll wait until it's just my husband and me (ha ha ha, that never happened). Finally I decided I'd just do it come what may. But grandma's china has to be taken out of the closet, unpacked, washed by hand, and then after we use them reverse the process. I was going to do it, I swear, but I just never had the time and on the two days I did I didn't have the energy. So I gave up on grandma's china.

Next, I was going to plate the food nice and do staging but it was already past the deadline and at dinner time everyone was ready to eat, no one wanted to wait for me to fancify their meal. Plus since we are being honest the hour before dinner is my grumpiest time of day. I don't know why, maybe because I don't snack between lunch and dinner, maybe because the stress of after school homework, piano, soccer, etc. slowly builds up to exploding as I think "and now after all that crazy I still have to make dinner that if I'm lucky half the family will like."

So my big plans to plate the meal failed, I did make sure we ate balanced meals most of the time but that's the best I could do. And I realized this exercise is about honoring, enjoying, and loving our food. So I took out my fancy glasses, poured in some delicious treats and pretended I was a princess.

It was fun! My kids loved it too. So now this is our new normal for M&M's and Skittles. For a moment I get to be royalty and escape the world... and then we get back to homework, piano, and making dinner.

Emily

I was excited by the idea that I could see where my food originated from. Excitement and anxiety. Would people be open to sharing how they do things?

Researching made me want to source back everything I eat and see just how they are made/processed. But also kind of disheartened that there wasn't already a real transparency when it comes to food. I loved visiting the U-pick farm and found that the operators were very open and willing to share what they know. It seemed like if the people operating and harvesting the food were more involved directly there was a sense of pride and more willingness to share and teach.

I wanted (and still do) to live within that veil of ignorance is happiness; trusting the advertisements and believing that what I'm eating is wonderful for me. Things that are pre-made and sold in packages in the center aisles at the grocery. But also fully grabbing onto the excitement and wonder of fresh produce in season and how wonderful that can be and taste. I've always loved being outside and curious about what was edible in different regions. So to see how a farm could grow a lot of just a few chosen produce, and get to pick it myself (from the plant!) was exciting.

Before the trip I felt great about food. During the trip I was in awe of certain foods — those grown on the farm. After the trip I really wanted to eat more apples and pumpkin. Trying to be more creative in how I could add them into meals somehow.

It was easier to enjoy the apples we picked knowing where they came from and how they care for their trees and farm in general. I am looking forward to the next time I eat! Though my thoughts lean more towards, is it fresh, do I need to unwrap it, should I eat this then? With a little bit of guilt because I do love me some parmesan Goldfish crackers, and Honeycomb cereal.

I really enjoyed looking into where my food comes from. Though I was frustrated in finding that the foods I was most curious about were the least transparent as to how they are processed and made. Which is probably due to a number of things. It's still annoying though. I'm sure the food industry has come a ways in requiring the nutritional information and ingredients. But I daydream about a time where every food website will have a short "how it's made clip" complete with sourcing ingredients. It almost makes me want to get out there and lobby for changes! Or just quit eating Oreos and move to Hawaii so I can grow my own cocoa.

Lisa

When I first received this assignment, I was surprised because of all the things I imagined your tasks to be like, this was not it. Then I wasn't sure what to do for the challenge as my family has chosen this type of service to do together so it wasn't something new or challenging for me. I thought about what to do and decided maybe there was some population or aspect that we hadn't served before and maybe I could reach out to them.

Homelessness is a big issue here in Utah. The areas downtown where the shelters are heavily policed because of increased violence in the area. There are many advocates working to solve some of the issues but it is unsettled right now. So I Googled (of course) ideas for helping the homeless in our area and discovered a lunch program for the family shelter. This program provides lunches for the children at the shelter that are not in school. The volunteer would provide lunches for 40 children. As a family, we discussed why we were doing this, about food in general, what our thoughts were about food, etc. to help bring more of a "food" aspect into this project instead of a "service" aspect. Following is some of my thoughts and feelings:

Abundance vs. lack - The first stop was Costco to purchase the lunch supplies. As we walked in and around the store, the absolute abundance of food available was overwhelming as I thought of who we were purchasing the lunch supplies for. Every day, I am surround by this abundance. I never lack food. Oh, sometimes I complain and wish I had a certain type of food. My pantry is filled to the brim with extra supplies: wheat, rice, canned goods, noodles, oil, tuna, etc. What would others think if they came into my pantry? Would they think I was a hoarder, glutton, selfish? My favorite stores to shop at tend to be small shops as the big stores overwhelm me, but this particular day at Costco, I was truly overwhelmed with all the food choices. Only a few minutes from our house, there were people who didn't always know where their next meal was coming from and I had this abundance before me. Food, and lots of it, is always around me and so much a part of my life. Questions that seemed of no importance were asked by each of us, "The organic juice is the same price as the regular should we get that?", "Do you think they like strawberry or raspberry better?", "Is this enough for them?", "Are they going to like these?" We left the store with our basket of stuff and nobody even blinked an eye that we were buying 8 bags of bagels and other supplies to feed 40 little children.

Because of this abundance I am surrounded by, I have used food as a comforter, solace maker, boredom buster, and to help me forget whatever is on my mind. Because of this abundance, I have a son who is incredibly picky and won't eat most things I make. He is willing to go without for a bit because he knows he will have plenty to choose from another time. Because of this abundance, we think it will always be there on the grocery shelves and on our own shelves. Because of this abundance, we forget where it came from and who physically provided it for us and who ultimately provides for us.

The lunch sacks - We lovingly prepared the lunches in paper sacks with stickers on them. I felt such a sense of gratitude we were able to do this. I wanted so much for the children to have success in life and hoped this little lunch brought them a slice of peace and happiness in their unstable world. This was a favorite part of the experience. The preparing, filling and packing of the lunch sacks was a fulfilling process for me. I was deeply grateful for this food and its purpose.

The shelter - I delivered the lunches to the shelter but because of privacy laws, I was not able to interact with the children themselves. The kindness of the homeless individuals in opening doors and assisting me was a humbling experience. I discussed food and food choices with the receptionist. She told me how excited the children get when they have these lunches, how fun it was for them to see what they got that day and how much the food was appreciated. Apparently, the children get tired of peanut butter (!) but eat what they are given because it is what is available. Again this idea of abundance and lack came to my mind.

The baby - The baby girl fit into the crook of her father's arm, was no more than a month old and had a cute pink bow in her hair. They came walking down the hall when I first entered the shelter. The father offered to help me with my boxes of lunches but I told him I could handle it as his load was more precious. As I left, I donned my sunglasses to keep the sun from my eyes but also to keep the tears hidden from the homeless on the sidewalk. I offered a prayer to heaven, "Please help that beautiful baby and her family to have the food and shelter they need. Give them the love and strength only thou can give them. Bless that little girl to grow up having the necessities she needs so she can be a force for good in the world."

Amber

This has been hard for me because I have the weirdest relationship with food. Ever since I can remember my mom was on some sort of diet. But I think I really started thinking about what I was eating after going to college and having the health and wellness class (which was required), I learned more about what is healthy and what is not. And during that time, I tried so hard to eat a certain amount of calories and I'd feel guilty any time I ate anything that wasn't considered "healthy." So then I'd eat more of the unhealthy. It was a yucky cycle. Then later, after kids and being overweight, I was introduced to Isagenix and the importance of cleanses. And how "fallen" our food really was. So once again I'd feel guilty for not following the regime perfectly or if I wanted to eat some sugar. I lost a lot of weight on that program but I also spent a lot of money.

So fast forward to today, I have been introduced to energy healing or what I like to call "faith work" and was taught that I could ask that my less than organic fruit and vegetables be changed to nourish my body for my greatest and highest good. But it brings up so many mixed emotions for me. Because I can see asking that for fruits and vegetables but when it comes to cakes or cookies or chocolate, it would seem that I'm trying to "change" something with almost next to nothing nutritional value into 3 cups of spinach. So I think I have "extreme" thinking. Maybe even black and white thinking.

But as I pray over my food and my kids' food and think about all the hands that prepared it and its journey through its beginning, it gives more "life" to my food and I am more grateful for it. I feel love and gratitude towards all the "hands" that prepared it. It makes the repetition of "Please bless this food to nourish and strengthen our bodies" have more meaning. I want to say, "Please bless this food to nourish and strengthen each and every one of our bodies and please bless that through our faith in the Atonement that its fallen state can be redeemed into something that will be for our greatest and highest good. Please bless it from its very beginning and all along its journey, bless all Thy creations that have taken part as it has made it to our table, we are truly grateful for it and for the variety of foods we have, for all the different tastes that help sustain us and keep us going on our mortal journey here."

Being able to be more intimate with the process of the food getting on my table has made me look at it differently, although I do feel like I have more healing to do to be more comfortable with any and all food placed before me. It makes me think of it differently. I think of how everything has a spirit and how those "spirits" that are a part of our food want to make us happy. Looking at it that way totally changes how I view food in general and all of God's creations. He has given us so many things to help us on our journey. Whether it's the crisp, yummy fruit and vegetables, or a warm fresh baked pie, they all have their place. I still think that moderation in all things applies; and as long as there is moderation, we can't go wrong.

{ Acknowledgements }

First and foremost, I give my thanks to God. For the opportunities He so graciously provides me with to stretch and progress, to become more like Him. He is the Master Teacher, and I'm eternally grateful for the lessons He creates just for me. This student is forever in His debt.

Thank you to my family. I am the mother to three beautiful children and the wife to one handsome husband. They are my everything. To Will, Elsie, and Tim — thanks for being so patient with me. Some of my greatest education begins with you. To my dearest Bradley, who has always been supportive of my crazy ideas and is my greatest cheerleader. Thanks for loving me so fully. Thank you Mom, for all the words you read and all the wisdom you share. Clarity often follows our conversations and allows me to process my countless thoughts. I wouldn't be where I am today without your guidance. And thanks to my mother-in-law who also graciously offers her time as a soundboard. I appreciate your calm assurance in my teaching abilities.

Many thanks go to many friends: Melisa, Amber, Allie, Nicola, Roni, Jennifer, Christi, Maria, Livia, Meggan, Felice, Margareta, Angie, Diana, Shanyn, Angela and many more. I could write a novel based on the ways you've helped me! Thank you for your continued encouragement, for positively pushing me onward and upward.

Thank you to everyone who held space for me to step into my gifts at the Quickening. And thanks to all the willing participants that bravely put these food experiences to the test and offered valuable feedback.

Additional Resources

Programs, Coaching, and Support Groups

- True Balance
  www.truebalancewithbeth.com
- The Quickening Movement
  www.quickeningevents.com
- Emily Ruth Coach
  www.emilyruthcoach.com
- Mindful Counseling
  www.mindfulcounselingutah.com
- Institute for the Psychology of Eating
  www.psychologyofeating.com
- Elevated Worldwide
  www.keepelevated.com
- Tree of Life Kundalini Yoga
  www.treeoflifekundaliniyoga.com
- Warriors Redeemed
  www.facebook.com/warriorsrEDeemED
- Embracing My Body
  www.facebook.com/groups/1823846247896994

Recommended Reading

- *Nourishing Wisdom: A Mind-Body Approach to Nutrition and Well-Being* by Marc David
- *The Slow Down Diet: Eating for Pleasure, Energy, and Weight Loss* by Marc David
- *The Gift of Our Compulsions: A Revolutionary Approach to Self-Acceptance and Healing* by Mary O'Malley
- *Health at Every Size: The Surprising Truth About Your Weight* by Linda Bacon
- *Intuitive Eating* by Evelyn Tribole and Elyse Resch
- *The Body Temple: Kundalini Yoga For Body Acceptance, Eating Disorders & Radical Self-Love* by Ramdesh Kaur
- *Whole Detox: A 21-Day Personalized Program to Break Through Barriers in Every Area of Your Life* by Deanna Minich
- *You Can Heal Your Life* by Louise Hay

Motivational Materials

- You Are Loved Designs
  www.youareloveddesigns.wordpress.com
- Emotional Mindfulness Card Deck
  www.thehealingcoach.com/emotional-mindfulness-card-deck.html
- Journaling to Recovery
  www.pickleboundbooks.com/products/journaling-to-recovery

Made in the USA
Lexington, KY
27 December 2017